"FINANCIAL PERFORMANCE ANALYSIS OF TRADING HOUSES IN INDIA"

BY

NEELAM MANHARBHAI PARMAR

LIST OF TABLE

SR.NO.	CONTAIN	PAGE NO
4.1	Current Ratio of Sampled Trading Houses	88
4.2	Abstract of F-Test	90
4.3	Result of F-Test	91
4.4	Quick Ratio of Sampled Trading Houses	93
4.5	Abstract of F-Test	94
4.6	Result of F-Test	95
4.7	Cash Ratio of Sampled Trading Houses	96
4.8	Abstract of F-Test	97
4.9	Result of F-Test	98
4.10	Interval Measure of Sampled Trading Houses	99
4.11	Abstract of F-Test	100
4.12	Result of F-Test	101
4.13	Net Working Capital Ratio of Sampled Trading Houses	102
4.14	Abstract of F-Test	103
4.15	Result of F-Test	104
4.16	Inventory Turnover Ratio of Sampled Trading Houses 188	106
4.17	Abstract of F-Test	107
4.18	Result of F-Test	108
4.19	Inventory to Working Capital Ratio of Sampled	109

	Trading Houses	
4.20	Abstract of F-Test	110
4.21	Result of F-Test	111
4.22	Debtors Turnover Ratio of Sampled Trading Houses	113
4.23	Abstract of F-Test	114
4.24	Result of F-Test	115
4.25	Average Collection Period of Sampled Trading Houses	117
4.26	Abstract of F-Test	118
4.27	Result of F-Test	119
4.28	Current Assets Turnover Ratio of Sampled Trading Houses	120
4.29	Abstract of F-Test	121
4.30	Result of F-Test	122

LIST OF ABBREVATION

SR.NO	ABBREVATION	FULL FORM
1	MMTC LTD	Metals and minerals trading corporation limited
2	PTC IND	Power trading corporation of india
3	STC INDIA	State trading corporation india
4	IND MOTOR PARTS	India motor parts and accessories ltd
5	CCL INT	Central coalfields limited
6	WH BRADY	William H. Brady
7	T.H	Trading houses
8	IMPO-EXPO	Import-export
9	NSE	National stock exchange
10	BSE	Bombay stock exchange
11	STARLITE COMPO	Starlite components
12	GAYATRI BIO	Gayatri bio organics ltd
13	MYSTIC ELECTR	Mystic electronics limited
14	EVA	Economic value added

CHAPTER: 1
OVERVIEW OF TRADING HOUSES AND SAMPLE PRFILE

OVERVIEW OF TRADING HOUSES AND SAMPLE PROFILE

INDEX

SR.NO	PARTICULARS	PAGE NO
1.1	INTRODUCTION	3
1.2	DEFINITIONS OF TRADING HOUSES	4
	OBJECTIVES OF TRADING HOUSES	5
1.4	CLASSIFICATION OF TRADING HOUSES	28
1.5	CRITERION FOR RECOGNITION OF TRADING HOUSES	29
1.6	FUNCTIONS OF TRADING HOUSES	31
1.7	ASSISTANCE/INCENTIVES OFFERED TO TRADING HOUSES BY GOVERNMENT OF INDIA ROLE OF TRADING HOUSES	32
1.8	SIGNIFICANCE OF TRADING HOUSES	38
1.9	SAMPLE PROFILE OF SELECTED TREDING HOUSES	38
1.10	CONCLUSION	44

1.1 INTRODUCTION

The comparative export performance of India, on the whole, was not satisfactory. The share of India in the total world exports fell from about 2 per cent in 1950 to 0.4 per cent in 1980. Since the mid eighties, there has, however, been some improvement. In 2012 it was 0.8 per cent and the target set by the Ministry of Commerce is one per cent by 2017. India was the 13th largest exporter in the world in 1950, but there are more than 30 countries above India now. Except for two years, in all the years. Since 1951, imports were larger than exports

India has experienced balance of payments problems of varying intensity in twenty nine out of thirty five years since the beginning of the second five year plan. The cost of India of this prolonged balance of payments problem, caused by the poor export performance has been heavy. The major drawbacks of India"s export sector are lack of integrated approach; problem recognition and action lags; technological problems; high costs; poor quality image; limited R&D and marketing research; supply constraints; faceless presence of Indian products abroad; infrastructural bottlenecks; structural weakness; uncertainties, procedural complexities and institutional rigidities; and inadequacy of trade information system.

From the beginning of the second five year plan (1956-61), the foreign exchange problem began to assume serious proportions. The Government began to realize the need for vigorous export promotion. It was very clear than concentrated efforts should be made for the promotion of the export of non-traditional items like engineering goods, iron and steel, iron ore, chemical & allied products, gems and jewellery, marine products, leather & leather manufacturers etc. It was also realized that unless positive steps were taken to build up a number of merchant houses, concentrating almost exclusively on exports and capable of undertaking trade on a sustained basis, it would be impossible to complete successfully against the highly experienced and resourceful trading house of other countries. resourceful trading house of other countries.

The importance of promoting merchant houses was further underlined by the need for providing channels for the export of the products of the small scale sector.

In September 1960, certain broad principles for recognition of export houses were formally adopted. The scheme of export houses has been modified a number of times thereafter.

An export house is a registered exporter holding a valid export house certificate issued by the director general of foreign trade. With a view to developing new products and new markets for exports, particularly from the small and cottage industries sector, a new scheme for the recognition of trading houses was introduced in 1981-

Trading houses are special category of export houses which have demonstrated export capabilities and have facilities for testing and quality control.

1.2 DEFINITIONS OF TRADING HOUSES

Trading Houses are of various types and forms. They exist in a number of countries and their activities and organization vary according to the historical background and the scenario in which they operate as well as national priorities and government policies. They are known by different names in different countries. So it is difficult to formulate a definition of Trading Houses which would be universally applicable. There are, however, resemblances in certain important aspects in the organizational structures of most of Trading Houses which make it possible for them to be analyzed as one generic entity. It is thus possible to describe activities, organization and definition of Trading Houses which would be universally applicable.

A definition that covers most cases is "Trading Houses are commercial intermediaries specialized in the long term development of trade in goods & services supplied by the other parties" they focus on exporting, importing and third country trading as their core activity and use overseas marketing organization and infrastructure as well as procurement networks to service suppliers and customers. They procure internationally and sell locally and they also procure internationally and sell internationally. They have flexibility and the agility to work in many markets with many products simultaneously as international marketing is their core business. They serve as commercial intermediaries between suppliers and buyers located in different countries.

Government of India has a scheme to recognize established exporters as Exports Houses, Trading House etc. Trading Houses are special category of exporters which enjoy export incentives granted by Government on exporting of goods & services.

A Trading House is defined as a registered exporter holding a valid and special category of export house certificate issued by the DGFT.

1.3 OBJECTIVES OF TRADING HOUSES

The important objectives of Trading Houses are:

- ❖ To operate itself as highly professional and dynamic institutions and act as important instruments of export growth
- ❖ To increase the relative profitability of the export business
- ❖ To provide necessary assistance to the new and small exporters & manufacturers to develop export business
- ❖ To provide marketing support for the development of exports
- ❖ To provide organizational and infrastructural facilities for development of exports
- ❖ To compensate the exporters for the high domestic cost of production
- ❖ To earn foreign exchange we need export earning to finance our imports.
- ❖ To generate employment opportunities
- ❖ To contribute to the overall development of the economy

The Trading Houses because of its size can obtain the benefits of economies of scale in purchasing, transporting, shipping, insuring and borrowing funds. A part of these benefits are passed on to the manufacturer/exporter for improving competitiveness.

1.4   CLASSIFICATION OF TRADING HOUSES

Classification of Trading Houses can be divided into two categories:
- I. Classification of Trading Houses on the basis of export performance level.
- II. Classification of Trading Houses on the basis of activity.

❖ Classification of Trading Houses on the basis of export performance level :-

Trading Houses are special category of export house. Merchant and manufacture exporters including those with foreign equity may apply for classification as Trading Houses and avail of special associated benefits. There are four such categories viz.

      I. Trading House

      II. Star Trading House

      III. Super Star Trading House

      IV. Golden Super Star Trading House

The applicant is required to achieve the prescribed average export performance level. The level of export performance for the purpose of recognition shall be as per the table below.

Classification of Trading Houses on the basis of activity:-

On the basis of activity, we may classify Trading Houses as under.

➢ Merchant Trading Houses :

The main aim of such firm is exporting of goods produced by other firms/companies. Such houses are not carry any manufacturing activities. They play an important role as merchant middlemen and exports goods & services on behalf of producer. As merchants, they buy and sell on their own account and earn a margin. They may also act as agents on behalf of the manufacturers or on behalf of the buyer and earn commission for their various services. They focus on exporting; importing and third country trading. They serve as commercial intermediaries between suppliers and buyers located in different countries. They have a network overseas for marketing and the experts at sourcing and procurement. They also have specialist departments providing expertise in trade support services. They provide essential value-adding services economically and they serve foreign customers as well as manufacturers. They operate with low margins on high volumes and make their profits mainly by quick and frequent turn around of funds. These companies have contributed substantially to the growth of foreign trade to the economic development of the country.

They focus on manufacturing of goods & services. The prime activities of manufacturer trading houses are production and marketing its products to domestic as well as foreign countries. They imports capital goods and raw materials, intermediates, components from the international market for own use only. Such Trading Houses export goods & services produced by itself only. They are not related with exporting of good produced by other firms/companies. In other word, manufacturer Trading Houses are not fall under the category of merchant or brokerage houses.

➤ Manufacturer & merchant Trading Houses :

They are engaged in manufacturing, exporting, importing and trading activities.

1.5 CRITERION FOR RECOGNITION OF TRADING HOUSES

The following are the criteria for grant of recognition as trading houses, star trading houses, super star trading houses, golden super star houses.

➤ Eligibility :

Merchant as well as manufacturer, exporters, service providers,export oriented units(EOUs) and units located in special economic zones(SEZs), agri export zone(AEZ's), electronic hardware technology parks(EHTS), software technology parks (STPs), bio technology parks(BTPs), units in small scale Industry/ tiny sector/ cottage sector and units registered with KV/Cs/KVIBs shall be eligible for supplying for status as Trading Houses.

➤ Value of Exports :

The criterion for recognition as trading house shall be on the goods and services, including software exports made directly, as well as on the basis of services rendered by the service provider during the preceding three licensing years or the preceding licensing year, at the option of the exporter. The exports made, both in free foreign exchange and in Indian Rupees, shall be taken into account for the purpose of recognition.

➢ **Export Performance Level :**

The applicant is required to achieve the prescribed average export performance level.

➢ **Deemed Exports :**

Deemed exports and exports of imports goods shall not be counted for export performance and not qualify for the purpose of recognition.

➢ **Exports made by subsidiary company :**

The exports made by a subsidiary of a limited company shall be counted towards export performance of the limited company for the purpose of recognition.

➢ **Exports made by small scale industries :**

Double Weightage is given to CIF or FOB earned by the export of products manufactured by small scale industries (SSI).

➢ **Exports made by the handlooms & handicraft sectors :**

Products manufactured by the handlooms and handicrafts sector, including hand – knitted carpet and silk products are given Double weightage on FOB earned by the export of such products; orTriple weightage on NFE earned by the export of such products.

➢ **Exports of sports goods :**

Double weightage is given on FOB earned by the export of sports goods

➢ **Export of goods manufactured in North Eastern States**

Goods manufactured by units located in North Eastern States shall be entitled for double force on FOB or NFE value of exports made for grant of trading house status.

➢ **Exports of agro products and horticulture produce:**

Exports of agro products like fruits and vegetables, floriculture and horticulture produce/products shall be entitled for double weightage on FOB or NFE value of exports made for grant of trading house status

1.6 FUNCTIONS OF TRADING HOUSES

Trading Houses are so important to all, discharge the following vital functions:

➢ **Market selection and market research**

Trading Houses have data bases and information networks as well as a presence in overseas markets. They use these continually to scan for opportunities worldwide. They search for demand/supply gaps, locate availability of finance, study the long-term plans of organization and governments, price trends and even political scenarios. They play a key role in monitoring the competition. These companies therefore know which product to sell where.

➢ **Customer identification and evolution**

The Trading Houses collect information about potential customers and their credit worthless, reliability and reputation. They closely study their customers, their current activities and future plans and make efforts to build with them relationship of confidence, trust and friendship.

➢ **Commercial and technical negotiations**

Trading Houses are efficient in making business offers through their marketing organization backed with their electronic databases, communication systems and networks. They have the experience and competence to carry out all the commercial work relating to export. The manufacturer makes the techno-commercial offer to the trading houses which then negotiates all the terms, secures the order, arranges delivery of the goods, pays the manufacturer and obtains the payment from the customer. Moreover the trading house"s presence in the overseas market enables it to obtain better prices and other terms.

> **Vendor development**

The Trading Houses also have an organization in the home country comprising of geographically dispersed regional facilities to facilitate vendor development and procurement. This organization identifies and develops manufacturers and also ensures that the long-term arrangements are satisfactory implemented.

> **Product/packaging adaptation and technology upgrading**

Trading House continually keep associate manufacturers informed about developments in foreign countries related to the technical features of the product, product techniques, design changes and packaging methods. For this service they use their overseas network and specialized product experts who are well traveled and who attend to international fairs and exhibitions.

> **Imports, particularly of items required for export production**

Trading Houses use their foreign offices and network for imports as well as for exports. They are able to negotiate favorable terms because of bulk buying and presence in the market. This helps manufacturers who generally require some imported components and materials for export production. Often these imported goods are stocked by the Trading Houses in customs bonded warehouses and supplied to the manufacturer when required.

> **Financial arrangements including securing credits**

Trading Houses borrow in bulk from financial institutions at comparatively low rates of interest and help to finance the transaction with cheaper funds. Trading Houses also provide financial assistance to the manufacturer though arranging deferred payments, financial guarantees and advance payments.

> **Counter-trading**

Counter-trade leverages governmental and sometimes other imports, to generate reciprocity by requiring foreign suppliers to buy products and services from the home country. Counter trade is best handled by Trading Houses because they have the size, range and infrastructure to deal with its diverse requirements. Counter-trade opens up new and large opportunities for manufacturers to have their products exported.

➤ Export documentation and shipping

Trade documents must be carefully prepared so that there are no problems in transportation, shipping, clearing, customs, obtaining payments as well as handling and subsequent claims. Trading Houses have well staffed and well equipped documentation and shipping departments and this is a major service provided to manufacturers. They have knowledge and experience which enables them to select the best modes of transport in terms of cost and quality of service. They can consolidate cargo which may often be going to its own warehouse overseas, thus lowering costs

➤ Protection against export risks including insurance

The risk in exports is a factor which adversely affect business of exporters. Trading Houses are continually involved in ascertaining the risks in foreign trade and know how to minimize these risk. They have gathered rich and varied experience as well as expertise in risk management which no single manufacturer/exporter would have been able to accumulate. With their established track records they get better terms from insuring organizations. Also they have access to expert advice on currency exchange rate. Fluctuations and are able to minimize these risks as well

➤ Ensuring payments

Collecting dues is a regular activity of Trading Houses for which they have specialties. In fact with their experience, databases and information networks, they are in a position to avoid the problem of bad debts. They are routinely in touch with major international credit rating agencies, banks etc., for checking out foreign customers. Again because of size they obtain these services at low rates.

➤ Dealing with claims

Since Trading Houses are committed to international trading on a long-term basis, they build credibility and a reputation for honoring their commitments, particularly with respect to quality and to avoid claims. However, if a claim is raised they will ensure that it is deal with promptly and efficiently. There are sometimes frivolous or unreasonable claims made by unscrupulous buyers. Trading Houses have the expertise and the clout to deal with such matters, thus providing much needed protection to the manufacturer. In many emerging economies and economies in transition there are bureaucratic hurdles involved in remitting funds abroad to settle claims or to re-import rejected goods. The governmental authorities are concerned that there could be misuses of this facility. Trading Houses, however are recognized by the government as a trusted organization with a stake in developing long-term trading and therefore manage to obtain such approvals and permissions with relative case.

➢ Managing crises and disasters

Export activity is dependent on number of variable factors. Many beyond the exporters control. This sometimes leads to unforeseen occurrences, for example, the inability of a supplier to deliver at the last moment resulting in the Trading Houses having to locate an alternative source or a buyer being unable to accept delivery of ordered goods requiring that an alternative customer be found soon. Trading Houses would have had experience of many such dangers and would have developed capabilities of declining with them. Disasters that could have sunk a manufacturer are managed by a Trading House.

➢ After-sale service and spare-parts availability

Trading Houses often export items that require after sale service. They will ensure that adequate arrangements for after-sale service, and stocking of spare-parts and repairs and maintenance are in place before they export such products. Often it is the Trading House itself which creates the facilities abroad for after-sale service. Manufacturers who associated with Trading Houses are therefore saved from expense and effort by getting at their disposal the after-sale service facilities arranged by the Trading House.

➢ Creating distribution network abroad

Trading Houses long-term involvement with exporting carefully chosen products to chosen markets makes it possible for them to go further than just doing one-off deals. In fact, even at the stage when the Trading House is preparing its market entry strategy for a product, it is already developing long-term plans for selling the product through appropriate distribution channels. It chooses suitable locally available channels. For certain products it could create its own channels including a warehouse for just-in-time delivery to customers.

➢ Project export, consortia and tender business

Trading Houses play a vital role when the foreign customers requirements is for goods and services to be supplied by a number of different organizations, often against a tender. Here the Trading House takes on the overall responsibility as principal and subcontracts the supply of various products and services to a number of companies including, if necessary, companies abroad. This is a function of the Trading Houses which is useful for a manufacturers because often the manufacturers would not even know about the existence of a tender, particularly if the tender pertained to a large project or supply of a range of products of which the manufacturers product formed only a small part. Moreover the chance of success is much greater if a manufacturer ties-up with a Trading House because of the latter's experience in dealing with project exports and tenders. Trading House is dealing with such business, continually and has developed the knock of assessing chances of success; it is unlikely to waste time and effort on bids that are not likely to succeed.

➢ Special relations with the government

Government use Trading Houses for achieving national goals. In many countries committed and trusted Trading Houses work closely with the governments in formulating and implementing the nations trading objectives. Some government export promotion schemes, such as those for helping small manufacturers to export, can be efficiently handled using the organizations of the Trading Houses. This helps governments as they can pass on some of the administrative and monitoring work to the Trading House which has the requisite expertise and infrastructure. Since Trading Houses are selected after checking their track records, they can relied upon to perform such tasks efficiently and with diligence.

1.7 Assistance/Incentives offered to Trading Houses by Government of India

➤ Assistance provided to Trading Houses by Government of India

The following are assistance that are provided to Trading Houses by Government of India.

➤ Production Assistance / Facilities

The important government measures related to export production are the following. Export processing zones(EPZs) were set up as enclaves separated from the domestic tariff area(DTA) by fiscal barriers and intended to provide an internationally competitive duty free environment. For export production at low cost, eight of the EPZs have since been converted into special economic zones(SEZs).

The export oriented units(EOUs) scheme, which is complementary to the EPZ scheme, was set up in 1981 under which a unit can be set up in any of the seven EPZs or at any other location in the country and be eligible for a host of liberal package of incentives which include same entitlements as given to EPZs.

In order to fully exploit the potential in the information technology (IT) sector and to promote IT related exports, the central government has set up software technology parks (100 per cent EOUs) since 1991.

To build a strong and efficient electronics industry with goods export potential, electronic hardware technology parks (EHTPs) were also set up.

➤ Financial Assistance

Financial assistance is given to the export sector mostly by the export-import bank of India, specified co-operative banks, commercial banks provide packing credit (Pre-shipment credit) at concessional rates. They also provide post-shipment credit. With the establishment of the Export-Import (Exim) bank in 1982, export Credit functions performed by the IDBI were transferred to the Exim bank. The export-import bank of India, set-up in 1982 by an Act of Parliament, for the purpose of financing, facilitating and promoting foreign trade of India, is the principal financial institution in the country for co-ordinating, working of institutions engaged in financing exports and imports. Exim banks plays a four-pronged role with regard to India's foreign trade: those of a co-ordinators, a source of finance, consultant and promoter.

➤ Marketing Assistance :

Some of the schemes and facilities which assist export marketing are mentioned below.

➤ Establishment of India Brand Equity Fund

Government of India initiated steps to establish an Indian Brand Equity Fund with the objective of promoting the made in India image abroad.

➤ Foreign Exchange

Foreign exchange is released for undertaking approved market development activities, such as participation in trade fairs and exhibitions, foreign travel for export promotion, advertisement & abroad market research, procurement of samples and technical information from abroad etc.

➤ Trade Fairs and Exhibitions

As trade fairs and exhibitions are effective media of promoting products, facilities are provided for enabling and encouraging participation of Indian exporters/manufacturer in such events. As mentioned earlier, foreign exchange is released for such purpose, the cost of participation is subsidized and the India Trade Promotion Organization (ITPO) plays an important role in organizing and facilitating participation in trade fairs/exhibitions. Besides the ITPO, some other promotional agencies also organize trade fairs. For example, the Marine Products Export Development Authority(MPEDA) organizes sea-foods trade fair, in India, in every 2nd year which attracts a number of foreign buyers and others connected with the sea-foods industry.

➤ Export Risk Insurance

The Export Credit Guarantee Corporation of India Ltd. (ECGC), a company wholly owned by Government of India and which functions under the administrative control of the Ministry of Commerce, has a number of schemes to cover several risks which are not covered by general insurers. The primary role of ECGC is to support and strengthen the export development of India by :providing a range of credit risk insurance covers to exporters against loss in of goods and services.offering guarantees to banks and financial institutions to enable exporters obtain better facilities from them.In other words, the objectives of ECGC are :

- To provide insurance cover to exporters against political and commercial risk

- To provide insurance cover to exporters against the risk of exchange rate fluctuations in respect of deferred payments.

- To provide insurance cover to banks against export credit and guarantees extended by them To provide insurance cover to Indian investors abroad against political risks.The covers issued by ECGC may be broadly divided into the following four groups.

- Standard policies issued to exporters to protect them against payment risks involved in exports on short-term credit.

- Specific policies designed to protect Indian firms against payment risks involved in exports on deferred terms of payment, services rendered to foreign parties construction works and turnkey projects undertaken abroad.Special Schemes.

➢ Quality Control and Pre-shipment Inspection

The international market is very competitive and quality of the export products is one of the important determinants of business. Inferior quality of exports damages the credibility of not only the exporter but also the nation. Hence, there shall not be any compromise on quality of exports. Exporters shall become quality conscious and the governments shall spare no efforts to assist quality improvements and to ensure that only products of satisfactory quality are shipped to foreign markets.

Pre-shipment inspection is the process of inspection of a batch of goods just prior to shipment to determine whether it satisfies the conditions for shipment, which may be concerned either with the quality weight, packaging, contraband character etc.

➢ Quality standards :

Standards or specifications of quality are pre-requisites of quality control because unless quality characteristics are assessed, specified and measured, quality control cannot be implemented. Sometimes, specifications are given by the buyer himself.

➢ Export quality control and inspection act, 1963 :

The Export (Quality Control and Inspection) Act, 1963, which is intended to provide for the sound development of the export trade of India through quality control and inspection and four matters connected therewith, empowers the central government to

Notify commodities which shall be subject to quality control or inspection or both prior to export;

Specify the type of quality control or inspection which will be applied to a notified commodity; Establish, adopt or recognize one or more standard specifications for a notified commodity,

➢ Institutional Assistance

Export marketing is assisted in different ways by a number of organizations. Some of autonomous bodies are mentioned below :

1. Commodity Boards
2. Export-Inspection Council
3. Indian Institute of Foreign Trade
4. Indian Institute of Packaging
5. Export Promotion Councils
6. Federation of Indian Export Organization
7. Indian Council of Arbitration
8. Marine Products Export Development Authority

Agricultural and Processed Food products Export Development Authority (APEDA) Indian Trade Promotion Organization

(B) Incentives provided to Trading Houses by Government of India:

The following are incentives that are provided to Trading Houses by Government of India.

➢ Town of Export Excellence :

A number of towns in specific geographical locations have emerged as dynamic industrial clusters contributing handsomely to India's exports. For example, Tirupur is exporting 80 per cent of its production of hosiery. It is consider industrial cluster towns such as Tirupur for hosiery, Panipat for woolen blankets, Ludhana for woolen knit wears to be eligible for the following benefits. Common service providers in these areas will be entitled for facility of EPCG scheme.

➢ Export Promotion Capital Goods Scheme :

The EPCG scheme allows import of capital goods for pre production, production and post production at 5 per cent customs duty subject to an export obligation equivalent to 8 times of duty saved on capital goods imported under EPCG scheme to be fulfilled over a period of 8 years reckoned from the date of issuance of license. Capital goods would be allowed at 0 per cent duty for exports of agricultural products and their value added variants. However, in respect of EPCG licenses with a duty saved of Rs. 100 crores or more, the same export obligation shall be required to be fulfilled over a period of 12 years.

➢ Target Plus Scheme :

The objective of the scheme is to accelerate growth in exports by rewarding star exports houses who have achieved a quantum growth in exports. High performing star export houses shall be entitled for a duty credit based on incremental exports substantially higher than the general annual export target fixed.

➢ Duty Exemption / Drawback:

The scheme of duty exemption is designed to avoid the incidence of commodity taxes like excise duty, customs duties on the exports so as to make the exports more price competitive. Customs duty and excise duty on inputs raise the cost of production in export industries and thereby affect the competitiveness of exports. Therefore, exporters needed to be compensated for the escalation in their costs attributable to such customs and excise duties. There are two types of drawback rates, viz..(a) all industry rate applicable to a group of products and (b) brand rate applicable to individual products not covered by the industry rate.

➢ Income Tax Exemption & Deductions :

The following exemptions and deductions are available to the exporters and other foreign exchange earners under the Income Tax Act, 1961.Deduction in respect of profits and gains from projects outside India (Sec.80HHB).Deduction in respect of export turnover (Sec. 80 HHC).Deduction in respect of earnings in convertible foreign exchange (Sec. 80 HHD).This facility will cease to be operative after close of financial year April 2010 to March 2011.

❖ ROLE OF TRADING HOUSES

The role of Trading Houses in international trade is very important. Trading Houses play an important role for the growth of exports and the dynamism of the export sector. India's total exports have been growing and the export sector has achieved some diversification and sophistication.Trading Houses are resourceful in terms of capital, skill, experience, exposure, ideas etc., are an assets which can contribute globalization of Indian business.So many small manufacturers and exporters are indirect exporters who exports through merchant exporters including Export/Trading houses and agents. Hence, the indirect export is more popular with firms which are just beginning their exporting and with those whose export business is small. In indirect export business, Trading Houses act as independent international marketing middlemen and take responsibility for the selling job on behalf of small Indian exporters.

The major advantage of exporting through Trading Houses is that a firm does not have to build up the infrastructure required for exporting and it does not have to bear the risks associated with international exports business.

The exporting activity involves several commercial and regulatory procedures. These procedures also involve considerable documentation requirements. Besides the documentation pertaining to the commercial aspects of the export business, there are documentation requirements of a regular in nature like excise clearance, foreign exchange regulations etc. The export documentation involved preparation of the specified number of copies of the prescribed documents pertaining to the different procedures. The exporting is special task and bundle of procedures which requires assistance from highly professional and dynamic institutions. Indian manufacturers with small export business are not in a position to build up infrastructure and expertise required for export activities. Further procedural complexities and delays in exporting activities are time and money consuming for small exporters. Trading Houses provide all such necessary infrastructure and act as international marketing middlemen and perform selling job of manufacturer.

Trading Houses are one of the important channels between the home country and the overseas market (exporters and buyers). Trading Houses fulfill complex export procedure on behalf of manufacturers. It also bears risks & responsibilities relating to exports and helps small exporters and manufacturers for international marketing of products and services. The Trading Houses is, therefore, often regarded as especially advantages for firms with small means and for those whose limited export business do not justify large investments in developing their own international marketing infrastructure. Trading houses provide necessary assistance to the new and infant exporters to develop export business. So, the Trading Houses play dominant role to broad base the export effort by co-opting small exporters.

By exporting through Trading Houses, manufacturers can benefit from Trading Houses, unrivalled knowledge of foreign markets. Trading Houses are specialized in export finance and management and can minimize financial risks. They are conversant with overseas buyer"s needs and market requirements. In addition, Trading Houses can tailor their services to the needs of manufacturers and buyers. They manage the risks associated with international trade transactions by establishing long-term business relationship with foreign clients and by carefully monitoring developments in overseas markets.

1.9 Significance of Trading Houses

Having a trading house develop certain specific markets can be extremely beneficial even for manufacturers who already have experience in exporting to a number of foreign markets. A trading house can help manufacturers: Save time since the Trading Houses already has well-established networking overseas.

Save money by spreading costs over several product lines. Benefit from the established credibility of the Trading Houses on foreign markets. Benefit from greater efficiency from the Trading Houses" experience in specific markets. Diversify their market and improve their export strategy. Minimize financial risks as Trading houses are specialized in export finance and management. Trading Houses have proven record of reliability for quality, prices and delivery of goods with long-term business perspective.

Trading Houses have global network for techno-commercial information. Benefit of better price realizations because of having overseas marketing organization.

All risks and hassles of exporting avoided with the help of Trading Houses.

1.10 SAMPLE PROFILE OF SELECTED TRADING HOUSES

SR.NO.	TRDING HOUSES	NET WORTH	CEO /MD/FOUNDERS
1	Adani Enterpris	8.7$ billion	Gautam Adani
2	MMTC Ltd.	1.5$ billion	Ved Prakash
3	PTC Ind.	10$ million	Pawan Singh
4	Swan energy	607 cr.	Nikhil v. merchant
5	Andrew Yule	3.8$ million	Shri debases jana
6	STC India	468 cr.	Rajiv Chopra
7	Shaily	124.34 cr.	Mike Sanghvi
8	Ind motor parts	687cr.	Pawan munjal
9	Uniphos ent	1$ million	RD shroff
10	Grandeur prod	500cr.	Vijay kumar deekonda
11	Control print	320cr.	Basant kabra
12	Apollo tricoat	370 cr.	Rahul gupta
13	Sat ind	700cr.	Prashant saraogi
14	Singer india	0.5$ million	Rajeev bajaj
15	Urja global	10$ million	Honey gupta
16	Competent auto	2$ million	Raj chopra
17	High ground ent	945 cr.	Sandeep r arrora
18	Cravatex	1$ billion	Rohan batra
19	Lahoti over	12$ million	Umesh rambilas
20	Tandl global	5$ million	Vineet bagana
21	Bombay cycle	975 cr.	Chirag c.doshi
22	Mishka exim	1$ million	Rejneesh gupta
23	ABans enterpris	496cr.	Abhishek bansal
24	Starlite compo	523cr.	Arvind bharti

25	CCL int	631cr.	Akash gupta
26	WH brady	333cr.	Pavan gokulchand morarka
27	Maximaa systems	251cr.	Manoj
28	Mystic electr	436 cr	Mohit khadiria
29	Gayatri bio	368 cr.	T. Sandeepkumar reddy
30	Empower india	2.4$ million	Zulfeqar mohammad khan

1 ADANI

TYPE	PUBLIC
INDUSTRY	CONGLOMERATE
FOUNDED	20 JULY 1988; 30 YEARS AGO
FOUNDER	GAUTAM ADANI
HEADQUARTERS	AHMEDABAD, GUJARAT INDIA
AREA SERVED	GLOBAL
KEY PEOPLE	GAUTAM ADANI (CHAIRMAN)

SERVICES	RESOURCES, LOGISTICS, ENERGY & AGRIBUSINESS
REVENUE	▲ US$ 11.357 BILLION (FY2017) [1]
TOTAL ASSETS	▲ US$ 27.032 BILLION (FY2017) [2]
DIVISIONS	ADANI ENTERPRISES LIMITED, ADANI PORTS & SEZ LIMITED, ADANI POWER, ADANI TRANSMISSION
WEBSITE	WWW.ADANI.COM

In April 2014, it added the fourth unit of 660 MW at its Tiroda Thermal Power Station, making Adani Power India's largest private power producer. In 2015, Adani was ranked India's most trusted infrastructure brand by The Brand Trust Report 2015. The Group operates mines in India, Indonesia and Australia and supplies coal to Bangladesh, China, and countries in Southeast Asia. The Group handled a total cargo of 168 million MT in 2016-17.

The company has contributed to the economy of Bunyu, North Kalimantan, Indonesia by producing 3.9 MMT of coal in 2016-17. The Group has made the largest investment by an Indian company in Australia at the controversial Carmichael coal mine, Galilee Basin, Queensland. It is estimated to produce coal at a peak capacity of 60 million metric tonnes per annum (MMTPA).[citation needed] The Group is the first in India to build a High-Voltage Direct Current (HVDC) system. In January, 2018, The Logistics and SEZ arm of the Group Adani Ports & SEZ Limited added equipment and machinery to render it the biggest dredger fleet in India.

❖ History

> First phase

The Adani Group commenced as a commodity trading firm in 1988 and diversified into the import and export of multi-basket commodities. With a capital of 5 lakhs, the company was established as a partnership firm with the flagship company, Adani Enterprises Limited, previously Adani Exports Limited. In 1990 the Adani Group developed its own port in Mundra to provide a base for its trading operations. It began construction at Mundra in 1995. In 1998, it became the top net foreign exchange earner for India Inc. The company began coal trading in 1999 followed by a joint venture in edible oil refining in 2000 with the formation of Adani Willmar.

> Second phase

The group's second phase started with the creation of large infrastructure assets. The company established a portfolio of ports, power plants, mines, ships and railway lines inside and outside India.

Adani handled 4 million Metric Tones (MT) of cargo at Mundra in 2002, becoming the largest private port in India. Later in 2006, the company became the largest coal importer in India with 11 million MT of coal handling. The company expanded its business in 2008 purchasing Bunyu Mine in Indonesia which has 180 million MT of coal reserves. In 2009 the firm began generating 330 MW of thermal power. It also built edible oil refining capacity in India of 2.2 million MT per annum. Adani Enterprises became the largest trading house in India importing coal with a market share 60%. It also supplies coal to NTPC Limited, India. The Adani group became India's largest private coal mining company after Adani Enterprises won the Orissa mine rights in 2010. Operations at the Port of Dahejcommenced in 2011 and ts capacity subsequently grew to 20 million MT. The company also bought Galilee Basin mine in Australia with 10.4 billion MT of coal reserves. It also commissioned 60 million MT of handling capacity for the coal import terminal in Mundra, making it the world's largest.In addition, in the same year, the Adani group also bought Abbot Pointport in Australia with 50 million MT of handling capacity. It commissioned India's largest solar power plant with a capacity 40 MW. As the firm achieved 3960 MW capacity, it became the largest private sector thermal In 2015 the Adani Group's Adani Renewable Energy Park signed a pact with the RajasthanGovernment for a 50:50 joint venture to set up India's largest solar park with a capacity of 10,000 MW. In November, 2015, the Adani group began construction at the port in Vizhinjam, Kerala.power producer in India. In 2012 The company shifted its focus on three business clusters - resources, logistics and energy.

Adani Power emerged as India's largest private power producer in 2014.Adani Power's total installed capacity then stood at 9,280 MW.The Mundra Port, Adani Ports and SEZ Ltd. (APSEZ), handled 100 million metric tonnes in fiscal 2013-14.On 16 May of the same year, Adani Ports acquired Dhamra Port on East coast of India for Rs 5,500 crore. Dhamra Port was a 50:50 joint venture between Tata Steel and L&T Infrastructure Development Projects, which has now been acquired by Adani Ports. The port began operations in May 2011 and handled a total cargo of 14.3 million MT in 2013-14. With the acquisition of Dhamra Port, the Group is planning to increase its capacity to over 200 million MT by 2020.

Adani Aero Defence signed a pact with Elbit-ISTAR and Alpha Design Technologies to work in the field of Unmanned Aircraft Systems (UAS) in India in 2016. In April, Adani Enterprises Limited secured approval from the Government of Gujarat to begin work on building a solar power equipment plant. In September, Adani Green Energy (Tamil Nadu), the renewable wing of the Adani Group, began operations in Kamuthi in Ramanathapuram, Tamil Nadu with a capacity of 648 megawatts (MW) at an estimated cost of Rs. 4,550 crore. In the same month, the Adani Group inaugurated a 648 MW single-location solar power plant. It was the world's largest solar power plant at the time in was set up In December, the Adani Group inaugurated a 100 MW solar power plant in Bhatinda, the largest in Punjab. The plant was built at a cost of Rs. 640 crore,on

22 December 2017 the Adani Group acquired reliance the power arm of Reliance Infrastructure for Rs 18,800 crore.

2 .MMTC LTD

Type	State-owned enterprise Public (MMTC)
Industry	Trading Company
Founded	26 September 1963
Headquarters	New Delhi, India
Key people	Mr. Ved Prakash[1] (Chairman & MD)
Website	MMTC Limited

MMTC is one of the two highest foreign exchange earner for India (after petroleum refining companies) It is the largest international trading company of India and the first public sector enterprise to be accorded the status of Five Star Export Houses by Government of India for long standing contribution to exportsBeing the largest player in bullion trade,

❖ History

➢ Foundation

The Company was incorporated on 26 September 1963 at New Delhi. The Corporation started functioning on 1 October. The main objectives of the company were export of mineral ores and import of essential metals. According to a latest news, MMTC is Asia"s biggest gold and silver importer.

➢ State Trading Corporation

After Independence the government decided to authorize the mining of scarce mineral resources to the public sector rather than private sector, although India's National Mineral Policy clearly states that it does not "preclude the State from securing the co-operation of private enterprise in the larger interest of the State or with a view to accelerating the pace of development" Under the Constitution of India, mineral rights and authority of mining laws remain vested with the state governments. On the other hand, Central government regulates the development of minerals under the Mines and Minerals (Regulation) Act of 1957.

The MMTC has its origins in the 1950s, when the Indian government, with the interest of boosting agricultural and industrial development, determined to earn valuable foreign currency through the export of canalized mineral ores, which the country had huge deposits of. As a consequence of the government's decision to earn foreign currency, the State Trading Corporation of India Ltd. was founded in 1956, as a wholly owned government subsidiary, to handle the export and import of selected commodities.

➢ 1963-2000

The Company had commenced its operation on 1 October 1963. With the rapid growth of the State Trading Corporation (STC) in its direct trading activities and in view of the importance given to the exports of mineral ores in the country's Five Year Plans, a decision was taken by the Government of India to split the STC and establish another corporation to deal exclusively with the trade in minerals and metals.

Japan and South Korea continued to be the major markets till the year of 1994. Then it made a foray into European market with the exports of one lakh tonnes of iron ore to Slovakia and Romania. Also in the same year, the company had commenced import of gold and silver against special import license for supply to the customers in the domestic area. Imports worth 20 metric tons of gold and silver worth 270 tonnes was made and the company opened new gold vaults at Hyderabad and vijag to offer its services to the customers in these areas. However, manganese ore exports remained depressed due to recession in the steel industry.

The wholly owned subsidiary MMTC Transnational Pte Ltd, Singapore was incorporated under the control of company in the year 1994 itself. During the year 1995, MMTC opened a duty-free jewellery show room at ChhatrapatiShivaji International Airport and a understanding was signed with the government of Orissa for development of existing Gopalpur minor port into an all-weather, deep water and direct berthing port. In the same year, Board for Industrial & Financial Reconstruction (BIFR) had approved the scheme of merger-cum-amalgamation of Mica Trading Corporation of India Limited (MITCO) with MMTC. From the year 1996 onwards, the company started to import the Chemical items and HomeopathicMedicines.orean companies for the supply of iron ore. In the identical year of 2003, the joint venture with the Orissa government namely NeelchalIspat Nigam Ltd was emerged as the second largest exporter of pig iron from the country.2012 On 14 September 2012. the Cabinet Committee on Economic Affairs decided disinvestment of 9.33% in MMTC.

3 PTC IND

Type	Public
Traded as	NASDAQ: PTC S&P 400 component
Industry	CAD/CAM/CAE/ PLMSoftware/ ALM/ SLM/ IOT
Founded	May 1985; 33 years ago
Headquarters	Needham, Massachusetts, United States
Key people	Robert P. Schechter (Chairman) James E. Heppelmann (President & CEO)
Products	PTC Creo, PTC Windchill, PTC MathCAD, PTC Integrity, PTC Servigistics, PTC Arbor text, ThingWorx
Revenue	▲ US$1.164 billion (2017)
Operating income	▲ US$40.9 million (2017)
Net income	▲ US$6.24 million (2017)
Total assets	▲ US$2.36 billion (2017)
Total equity	▲ US$885.4 million (2017)
Number of employees	6,041 (2017)
Website	ptc.com

❖ **Products &Services**

PTC has five product segments under two divisions: IoT Group and Solutions Group. The IoT Group consists of its Internet of Things and Augmented Reality business units and the Solutions Group includes CAD, PLM, and SLM.

❖ History

➢ Early History

The Russian immigrant and mathematician Dr. Samuel Ginsberg worked at software-design providers Applicant and Computer vision (acquired by PTC in 1998) prior to forming Parametric Technology Corporation in May 1985. In 1988, the company unveiled its first commercial product called Pro/ENGINEER and soon-after landed John Deere as its first customer. Pro/ENGINEER was the first parametric, feature-based solids modeling CAD software. Pro/ENGINEER could recognize a change in a single variable of a design and adjust the rest of the model accordingly.

Paramedic"s revenue grew quickly from $3m in 1988 to $45m in 1991. The company officially went public in 1989 under the stock ticker PMTC. Parametric continued to gain industry recognition in 1992 with Industry Week naming Pro/ENGINEER „Technology of the Year" and the company landing its largest customer to-date, Caterpillar. It made the Fortune 500 in 1995 and exceeded $800m in revenue in 1997. The company made a few acquisitions in the 1990s including CDRS and 3DPaint products from Evans & Sutherland, Rasna Corp., Reflex and Division Group.

In 1998, Parametric acquired the company (Computer vision) its founder (Dr. Ginsberg) had previously worked for. The company consequently acquired Computer vision subsidiaries including Wind-chill Technology, a Minnesota-based startup co-founded by current PTC CEO, James Heppelmann. Later that year, Parametric shipped Wind-chill, an internet-based solution for Product Lifecycle Management (PLM). PTC announced in 1999 it had 25,000 customers across aerospace, retail/footwear/apparel, automotive, industrial equipment, consumer products, electronics, and high-tech industries.

In the 2000s, Parametric developed lifecycle management software for products, assets, applications, processes and services through acquiring several companies including Polyp an Technologies, Arbor text, Apt avis Technology Corp (Retail PLM), NetRegulus, Synapses Technology, Relax Software and Planet Metrics. It also made a few CAD-related acquisitions including Captain, NC Graphics, Math soft (developers of MathCAD), ITEDO Software GmbH and Concrete.

➢ Recent History

On October 1st, 2010, James Heppelmann assumed the role of President and Chief Executive Officer of Parametric. The company renamed its initial CAD product Pro/ENGINEER to PTC Creo. The company officially changed its legal name „Parametric Technology Corporation" to PTC Inc and its NASDAQ ticker to „PTC" from „PMTC" in 2013. PTC continued to acquire CAD and PLM-related companies including MKS Software, 4CS Software Solutions, Servigistics, Enigma, Net IDEAS, Antigo and Plugin76. In December 2013, the company made its preliminary Internet of Things acquisition with the $112m takeover ThingWorx. PTC continued to acquire IoT companies with the acquisition of IoT connectivity management provider Axeda Corporation for $170m in August 2014, IoT predictive analytics company Cold light for $105m in May 2015 and industrial connectivity provider Kepware for $100m in January 2016. The company made its initial outside investment into the Augmented Reality space with the acquisition of Vitoria from Qualcomm in November 2015 and then acquired Waypoint Labs in April 2018.

Rockwell Automation made a $1bn equity investment in PTC acquiring 8.4% ownership stake in PTC on June 11, 2018. PTC also announced major strategic partnerships with ANSYS and Microsoft in 2018.

1985 - Company founded by Samuel Geisberg, formerly from Prime Computer, Computer vision, and Applicant.

1988 - Steve Walske named CEO. Company shipped Pro/ENGINEER and was considered first to market with modeling design software.] This positions PTC as a leader in the CAD industry until the mid-1990s when a new generation of low-cost competitors arrive in the market.

1989 - Initial public offering

1992 - Caterpillar Inc. becomes PTC"s largest customer.

1996 - PTC acquires Reflex project modeling and management software technology sold the following year to the Beck Group.

1998 - Company ships Wind-chill and is considered first to market with internet-based solutions for Product Lifecycle Management(PLM). PTC acquires Computer visionCorp.

1999 - PTC announces it has 25,000 customers. Major industries include aerospace, retail/footwear/apparel, automotive, industrial equipment, consumer products, electronics, and high tech.

1999 - Acquired Division Group (Division Ltd, Bristol Uk, Division Inc) Virtual reality - division Head Mounted Display & Software

2002 - The company releases Pro/ENGINEER Wildfire. This is the first CAD system to support web-based services.

2005 - Acquired Arbortext for technical publishing technology. Acquired Aptavis for retail, footwear and apparel technology.

2006 - Acquired Math soft for its engineering calculation software. Acquired ITEDO for its 3D technical illutretation software.

2007 - Acquired CoCreate for its direct modeling technology.

2008 - Acquired Synapsis for its performance analytics technology to improve environmental performance of products.

2009 - Acquired Relex Software for its reliability engineering software.

2010 - James E. Heppelmann announced as CEO effective October 1, 2010. Company renames Pro/ENGINEER to PTC Creo and promises the market product design software that is scalable, open, and easy-to-use.

2011 - Acquired 4CS for its warranty, service, support and service parts technology. Acquired MKS for its application lifecycle management technology for all software development processes.

2012 - Acquired Servigistics for its suite of service lifecycle management software.

2013 - Acquired Net IDEAS hosting vendor for more technology deployment options. Acquired Enigma for its ability to deliver technical content to aftermarket service environments. Acquired Things platform developer ThingWorx for their software applications that connect and track network-enabled products.

2013 - Acquired ThingWorx, the Exton, Pennsylvania-based creators of an award-winning platform for building and running applications for the Internet of Things (IoT).

2013 - The company changed its legal name from Parametric Technology Corporation to PTC Inc.

2013 - The company changed its NASDAQ ticker symbol to "PTC" from "PMTC".

2014 - Acquired Axeda Corporation

2014 - Acquired ATEGO Software, a leader in MBSE (model-based systems engineering) tool used in aerospace, transportation, and automotive industries (such as Alstom Transport and Rolls-Royce Defense)

2015 - Acquired the Euphoria business from Qualcomm Connected Experiences, Inc., a subsidiary of Qualcomm Incorporated. The Euphoria platform is an augmented reality (AR) technology platform.

2015 - Acquired Kepware, a software development company that provides communications connectivity to industrial automation environments.

4 ANDREW YULE

Type	Government-owned corporation
Founded	1863
Founder	Andrew Yule
Headquarters	Kolkata, India
Key people	Shri Debasis Jana [(Chairman and Managing Director)]
Net income	₹27 crore(US$3.8 million) (2016-17)[1]
Owner	Government of India
Parent	Yule Group
Divisions	Engineering, Electrical, Tea

Subsidiaries	Hooghly Printing
Website	www.andrewyule.com

❖ History

The business was founded by Andrew Yule in 1863 and incorporated as a private company in 1919. During British Raj the company was a large conglomerate. The company had varied and diversified business interests ranging from jute, cotton, coal, tea, engineering, electrical, power, chemicals, insurance, railways, shipping, paper, printing apart from maintaining a zamindari and managing house of several companies in India. The company was managed by Andrew Yule and his brother George Yule and later by David Yule. The Bengal Coal Co was part of Andrew Yule group holding collieries in Bengal & Bihar. The company was turned into a public company in 1948, after India's independence from the British Empire. It became a central public sector enterprise (CPSE) (schedule B company) in 1979, after the Indian government completed a series of equity share acquisitions (49% in 1974 and 2% in 1979). As of 2011, the shareholders are the Indian government (97.46%), Financial Institutions (0.33%), and the remainder publicly traded (2.21%).

5. STC INDIA

The 1990s saw a tremendous rise in the number of technical communication professionals in India. With no formal education in the field of technical communication, the need for a forum to exchange ideas as well as share experience and knowledge was badly felt.

Gurudutt Kamath started a Technical Writing Mailing list that served as an instrument for like minded professionals in spirit of technical communication to form a chapter – STC India. This list and meetings of technical communicators in various cities brought together the few STC members in India. By 1998, active discussions began on the need for establishing an Indian STC Chapter. Soon, Gurudutt Kamath circulated an STC application form that was signed by 17 members and submitted for approval by STC. The first Administrative Council took charge with Gurudutt Kamath as the Chapter President in 1999.

Since then, the India chapter has increased its strength to around 100 registered members and several sustaining member organizations. STC India Chapter plays a key role in educating technical communication professionals in the country through learning sessions that impart information about the skills required to shape their careers.

6. SHAILY INDIA

Shaily Engineering Plastics Ltd., is a quality supplier of high precision injection molded plastic components, subassemblies & assemblies for various OEM requirements. SEPL is certified to ISO: 9001:2008, ISO/TS 16949:2009, ISO 15378:2011, ISO 13485:2012 quality certifications and is the first injection molding company to have obtained the ISO: TS16949 certification in India.

SEPL has 5 manufacturing plants located near Baroda, Gujarat, India with 100+ injection molding machines with clamping force between 35T – 1000T including 3

Injection Blow Molding machines. The plants are equipped with various post molding facilities viz., hot stamping, ultrasonic welding, Vibration Welding, vacuum metalizing, pad printing, Screen printing, Painting, hot foiling, Laser Marking, manual assembly lines, semi-auto assembly lines and fully automated assembly lines & other post molding services.

The company has been exporting components, sub-assemblies & assemblies to customers in US, Europe & Middle East since past more than 20 years and is 100% compliant to the quality standards & logistics requirements of these customers.

7. IND MOTOR PARTS

India Motor Parts & Accessories Limited (**IMPAL**) a TVS Group Company was incorporated on 12th July 1954. The Company is engaged in the distribution of automobile spare parts and accessories through its 50+ branch network representing over 50 manufacturers. IMPAL is one of the few all India distributors of motor parts and deals in engine group components, brake systems, fasteners, radiators, suspensions, axles, auto electrical, wheels, steering linkages, instrument clusters etc.

8. UNIPHOS ENT

Industry	Gas Detection, Engineering
Founded	1993
Founder	Rajju Shroff
Headquarters	Mumbai, India
Key people	Rajju Shroff, CMD - Rahul Singh, Vice President (Business)
Services	Gas Detection, Fumigation, Breathalyzer, CEMS, TOC Analyzer, COD Analyzer, Engineering
Website	www.uniphos-she.com

9. GRANDEUR PROD

M/s. Grandeur Products Limited was established in 1983 and started its operations in Kolkata, West Bengal. The Company is in the business of FMCG projects particularly into Coffee and related products. Grandeur Products Limited is led by a group of professionals from diverse and rich background, who are fully prepared to take the challenges of tomorrow marketplace. With our primary focus on Quality, Long term client relations and Obtaining a trusted name in the industry. Grandeur Products Limited strongly believes in contributing towards the betterment of society and endeavours to create a positive impact, while achieving its business goals.

10. CONTROL PRINT

As a consumer every single day our work touches you in small & large ways. The Food, Beverage, Pharmaceutical, and FMCG/Personal Care industries rely upon us to provide necessary statutory information such as Best Before Codes and Maximum Retail Price information. Several industries such as Pipe & Plastic, Wire & Cable, Steel & Metal, Cement, Plywood…. Rely upon us to provide necessary product information such as thickness, pressure ratings, heat numbers… on their products. And all manufacturing industries require high levels of traceability using Batch Codes, Serial Numbers, or Variable Barcodes to track & trace their products across their entire supply chain.

So the next time you look at a best before date, the specification of your speaker wire, the thickness and coating of your glass sheet… its very likely that as one of the key providers of Coding & Marking Solutions, that are used by almost every manufacturing industry in order to print any type of variable information directly onto their productions lines, you are looking at one of our codes.

11. APOLLO TRICOAT

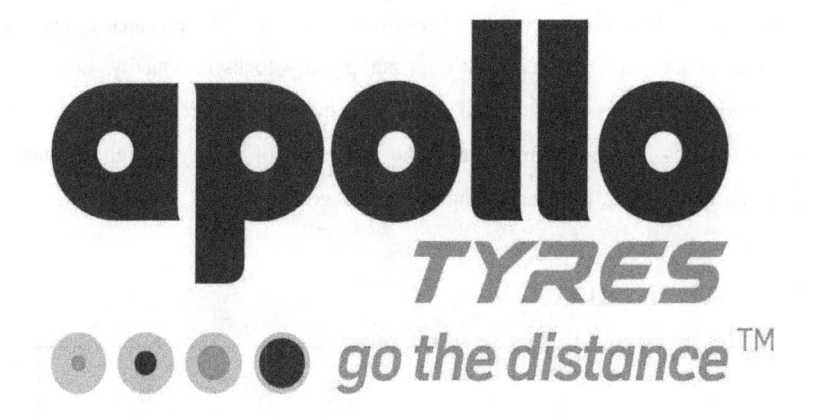

Type	Public company
Traded as	NSE: APOLLOTYRE BSE: 500877
Industry	Tyres

Founded	1972[1]
Headquarters	Gurgaon, Haryana, India[2]
Key people	Onkar Singh Kanwar(Chairman and MD) NeerajKanwar (Vice Chairman & MD)
Revenue	₹146. 74 billion (US$2.28 billion) [3]
Number of employees	16000
Website	http://www.apollotyres.com

It gets 69% of its revenues from India, 26% from Europe and 5% from other geographies.

Apollo announced its entry into the two-wheeler tyre segment with contract manufacturing in March 2016. In November 2016, the company signed a MoU with the Government of Andhra Pradesh to set up a new factory in Andhra Pradesh to manufacture tyres for two-wheelers and pick-up trucks.The company's second plant in Europe was inaugurated by the Hungarian Prime Minister, Viktor Orban, on April 2017.

❖ History

Apollo Tyres Ltd. was incorporated on 28 September 1972 as a Public Limited Company and obtained certificate of Commencement of Business on 24 October, 1972. The Company was promoted by Bharat Steel Tubes, Ltd. Raunaq International Pvt. Ltd., Raunaq& Co. Pvt. Ltd., Raunaq Singh, Mathew T. Marattukalam and Jacob Thomas . In 1975, the company made its Initial public offer of equity shares and its first manufacturing facility was commissioned in Perambra Plant, Thissur, Kerala, India in 1977, followed by its 2nd plant at Limda, Gujarat, India in 1991. The company acquired Premier Tyres Limited- PTL in 1995, which became its 3rd plant at Kalamassery, Kerala, India. In 2008, it started a new plant at Chennai Tamil Nadu, India. A year later in 2009, the company acquired the Netherlands-based tyre maker VredesteinBanden B.V.(VBBV) for an undisclosed sum.

The company focused on the production of truck tyres in India and introduced its first truck tyre, Rajdhani in India. The company expanded its operation across Indian and, in 1996, it expanded operations outside India by acquiring Dunlop's Africa operations. In 2013, it disposed off the Dunlop brand in Africa along with most of the South African operation in a sale to Sumitomo Rubber Industries of Japan.] The very same year, it started its Global R&D Centre, Europe in Enschede, the Netharlands.

In 2015, Apollo Tyres bought Germany's Reifencom for €45.6 million. It shifted its corporate office for Europe region to Amsterdam from Enschede, the Netherlands and opened a Global R&D Centre, Asia in Chennai, India a few months later.

In 2016, the company signed an MoU with the government of Andhra Pradesh to set up a new factory in the state. In 2017, it inaugurated its plant in Hungary. On 9 January 2018, the Chief Minister of Andhra Pradesh, N Chandrababu Naidu laid the foundation stone for Apollo Tyres' ₹1,800 -crore tyre factory in Andhra Pradesh. The plant will come up over a 200-acre site in Chinnapanduru village near Sri City in Chittoor district and produce passenger car radial (PCR) tyres with an initial capacity of 5.5 million tyres per year and will serve both domestic and export markets.

12.SAT ind.13.singer india,Headquarters: India, Founded: 1977 Parent organization: Retail Holdings ,14.urja global ,15.competent auto,16.high ground ent.17.cravatex,18.lahoti over, 19.Tandl global ,20.bombay cycle ,21.mishka exim,22.abans enterpris,23.starlite compo,24.CCL int.25.WH brady, 26.WH brady Headquarters: India Founded: 1895 ,27.maximaa systems, 28.mystic electr ,29.gayatri bio ,30.empower india, Headquarters: India Founded: 1981 these are the companies which are included in my company profile of data net worth and the rpime information about these company and the data i have mention in the above information and also i have analysed the data analysis in this particular research in below chapters.

1.11 Conclusion

This chapter deals with introduction, definitions of Trading Houses, types, classification, functions, objectives, significance of Trading Houses in India. It also gives criteria for recognition of Trading Houses, assistance and incentives provided to Trading Houses by Government of India and role of Trading Houses in India.

References:

I. Francis, Cherunilam. "*Business Environment*", Himalaya Publishing House, Delhi.
II. www.oath.on.ca.
III. Foreign Trade Policy of Govt. of India - www.exim.indiamart.com.
IV. Federation of Indian Export Organization, Ministry of Commerce,
V. Govt. of India, New Delhi.
VI. www.oath.on.ca.
VII. Ministry of Commerce and Industries, Department of Commerce,
VIII. Udyog Bhavan - New Delhi 110 011.
IX. Center for Monitoring Indian Economy Francis, Cherunilam. "*International Trade and Export Management*", Himalaya Publishing House, Delhi. National Informatics Centre - New Delhi

CHAPTER: 2
AN OVERVIEW OF FINANCIAL ANALYSIS

INDEX

SR.NO	CONTAIN	PAGE NO.
2.1	INTRODUCTION	47
2.2	PROCESS OF FINANCIAL ANALYSIS	48
2.3	METHODS OF FINANCIAL ANALYSIS	50
2.4	STAKE HOLDERS OF BUSINESS	51
2.5	TECHNIQUES \ TOOLS TO MEASURE FINANCIAL PERFORMANCE	52
	(A) OLD TOOLS I. RATIO ANALYSIS II.. FINANCIAL STATEMENT ANALYSIS III. DU PONT ANALYSIS	53
	(B). MORDEN TOOLS I.EVA (ECONOMIC VALUE ADDED) II.BALANCED SCORE CARD	75
❖	REFERNECE	

2.1. INTRODUCTION

Business is an activity which functions with various factors. Business is the pool of activities and all the activities can run with the fund. Without fund business is not possible. in the present scenario of business can be possible with debt fund means any businessman can start the business with own fund and debt fund but the condition is that only to return the debt fund with in time. So, it is possible to do the business with debt fund. This debt fund available from the various sources, which are easily available, Now the question raised that why such sources provides fund to you?

The reason behind they return from the investment once any investor provides fund they wants return in time and with growth. So, being investor if you are going to invest money there is need to exercise that such company's financial result is profitable or not and to do the financial analysis is possible with the help of various accounting tools.

However, it is to be noted that fundamentally, the balance sheet indicates the financial position of the company as on that point of time. However, profit and loss account is a statement, which is prepared for a particular financial year. In Indian context, where an analyst has to rely upon the audited financial statement for a particular company, the performance is to be judged from the financial statement only. This chapter however indicates some of the techniques, which can be used for such Usefulness of financial performance to various stakeholders.The analysis of financial performance is used by most of the business communities. They include the following.

2.2. PROCESS OF FINANCIAL ANALYSIS:

The information for financial analysis and appraisal essentially emerge from financial statements. Such analysis covers:

(1) Segregating of character additives of financial statements and organizations of distinctive factors duly described in order that the computation can be actually ascertained for checking and accuracy. The facts contained inside the income statement and the balance sheet are to be completely recast and offered in a condensed and unified form.

(2) to set up extensive relationships between the individual additives of Income statement and Balance sheet. This is done thru utility of the tools and strategies of financial analysis.

(3) Assessment and interpretation of the comparative data acquired via application of the gear of financial evaluation

The evaluation and interpretation of financial statements constitute the ultimate of four essential steps of accounting. The first 3 steps involve: (1) evaluation of every transaction to determine the accounts to be debited and credited and the size or valuation of every transaction to determine the quantities involved. (2) Recording the information in books of original entry, summarization in ledger, and preparation of a trial balance. (3) Preparation of financial statements. The fourth step of accounting – the evaluation and interpretation of financial statements – outcomes within the presentation of information a good way to aid business executives, traders and creditors. The process of analyzing financial statements entails the compilation and study of economic and operating data and the preparation and interpretation of measuring devices along with ratios, trends and percentages. . Evaluation of statements consists in keeping apart information consistent with some specific plan, arranging them in corporations in line with positive characteristics, after which offering them in a convenient and without problems read and understandable form. On this manner the analyst attempts to decide the importance and that means of the financial statement data.

The financial statement figures consist now not simplest of account balances, which commonly are the result of many debit and credit entries for a spread of transactions, however additionally mixtures of account balances. As a result, the figures frequently do now not represent homogenous records. The accounting data is the result of limitless transactions taking region right from beginning of the ledger till the last date of the accounting year. For correct interpretation, many a instances this requires for evaluation of the data. As an instance, the claims of a firm towards income made are quantified below the top of debtors. However this absolute figure won't be of much utility within the feel that it is applicable to confirm the position of borrowers who've no longer paid for final 30 days, 60 days, 120 days, a 180days s and so forth. Such information handiest could be more significant to the management of the company for taking a suitable decision. Interpretation requires comparison also. Mere examination of the components of a statement can't be expected to lead to exact conclusions in regard to the financial fame of a organisation. After the financial statement has been has been dissected into its parts, it's very important to degree the relative magnitudes of the various items. As an example, the current liabilities of a business at a selected date is a particular amount, and an opinion is desired as to whether it is probable that the firm may be able to meet these duties, the amount of the liabilities may be as compared with the amount of assets that the business has to be had to pay them : the cash and such assets as receivables and the products to be able to be transformed into cash in the ordinary operation of the firm for the duration of the approaching year. If this amount is higher, the analyst might probably do not forget the debt-paying capability of the firm pleasant. But, on getting older the amounts payable and receivable, if it is observed that current liabilities becomedue earlier than a sufficient amount of money might be obtained from clients to pay them, the scenario turns to be unsatisfactory.

It is thus seen that in order to interpret the position of an enterprise it is necessary not only to separate the totals given in its financial statements into their components but also to make comparisons of the various components and to examine their content. Adding to the content, a study of the changes that have befell in the firm many periods ought to be made. This sort of study is carried out by using analyzing the tendencies of the numerous critical factors in a sequence of statements. Financial statement analysis is, therefore, in large part a study of relationships among the financial elements in a business, as disclosed by a single set of statements, and of the tendencies of those factors, as shown in a sequence of statements.

2.3 METHODS OF FINANCIAL ANALYSIS:

The analysis and interpretation of financial statements tries to decide the meaning and importance of the financial data to check the performance in beyond, forecast for the future business performance and verifying the financial stability of the firm. In other words, financial evaluation is the assessment of a company's past, present and anticipated financial performance and financial situation. The main objective of financial analysis is to identification firm's financial strengths and weaknesses and to provide the basic foundation for financial decision making and planning. There are different methods of analysis. Such as:

(1) Horizontal analysis: that is the assessment, evaluation and interpretation of similar items of financial statements regarding different accounting periods.

(2) Vertical analysis: that is contrast, evaluation and interpretation of two items or variables of financial statements referring to the same accounting period.

(3) Static and dynamic analysis: Static analysis measures the relationships in some of the items in a single set of statements. Dynamic analysis measures the adjustments in such items in successive statements. Static analysis is vertical analysis and dynamic analysis is horizontal analysis.

(4)Internal and external Analysis: The internal analysis is done by the organization to take the decision internally with the help of financial data. In external analysis decision making is done by the outsiders like investors, banker, government revenue authority, any creditor, customers and other.

2.4 STAKEHOLDERES OF BUSINESS

1. Trade Creditors

The creditors provide goods / services on credit to the firm. They always face concern about recovery of their money. The creditors are always keen to know about the liquidity position of the firm. Thus, the financial performance parameters for them evolve around short term liquidity condition of the firm.

2. Suppliers of long term debt

The suppliers of long term debt provide finance for the on-going /expansion projects of the firm. The long term debt providers will always focus upon the solvency condition and survival of the business. Their confidence in the firm is of utmost importance as they are providing finance for a longer period of time. Thus, for them the financial performance parameters evolve around the following:

i) Firm's profitability over a period of time.
ii) Firm's ability to generate cash - to be able to pay interest and
iii) Firm's ability to generate cash – to be able to repay the principal and
iv) The relationship between various sources of funds.

The long term creditors do consider the historical financial statements for the financial performance.

However, the financial institutions \ bank also depends a lot on the projected financial statements indicating performance of the firm. Normally, the projections are prepared on the basis of expected capacity expansion, projected level of production \ service and market trends for the price movements of the raw material as well as finished goods.

3. Investors

Investors are the persons who have invested their money in the equity share capital of the firm. They are the most concerned community as they have also taken risk of investments – expecting a better financial performance of the firm. The investors' community always put more confidence in firm's steady growth in earnings. They judge the performance of the company by analyzing firm's present and future profitability, revenue stream and risk position.

4. Management

Management for a firm is always keen on financial analysis. It is ultimately the responsibility of the management to look at the most effective utilization of the resources. Management always tries to match effective balance between the asset liability management, effective risk management and short-term and long-term solvency condition.

2.5 TECHNIQUES \ TOOLS TO MEASURE FINANCIAL PERFORMANCE

There is various users study the financial statement for different aspect for the analysis of financial statement and use various tools and techniques which are available, right now there are some old tools and some new tools available for the analysis of the financial statement in which:

A. Old tools covers
    I. Ratio analysis
    II. Financial statement analysis with the
        1) Comparative statement
        2) Common size statement analysis
        3) Trend analysis
    III. Du pont analysis

B. Morden tools covers
    1) EVA (Economics value added)
    2) Balanced score card

(A) OLD TOOLS COVERS

I. RATIO ANALYSIS

Ratios are calculated based on the financial and related statement like. Profit &Loss account, Balance Sheet etc.

The ratios are classified as under 5:
❖ Leverage Ratios

c)	Activity Ratios And
d)	Profitability Ratios

The objective behind calculating each of the ratios is different and the outcome expected is also different. Let us study the objective behind every type and sub-type of ratio.

a) Liquidity Ratios

Liquidity Ratios are calculated to measure the firm's ability to meet its current obligations. The solvency position is indicated by the liquidity ratios. The solvency position is very critical for any firm. It is often indicated by the Indian industry that it has ample sources available for the long term finance, but very limited sources are available for the short term finance or to meet working capital requirement. So, a firm's performance in this area is an important indication towards the performance.
The following are the ratios that indicate liquidity position.

i)Current Ratio

Current Ratio is calculated by dividing current assets by Current Liabilities. The forma for the Current Ratio is as under:

Current Ratio =	Current Assets
	Current Liabilities

Where…

Current Assets include cash and those assets which are convertible into cash within a period of one year. Current Liabilities includes all obligations which are to maturing within a period of one year.

ii) Quick Ratio

It is also popularly known as an acid test ratio. This ratio normally describes the quick or liquid assets and current liabilities.

It is considered that an asset is liquid if it can be converted into cash immediately. Cash is considered to be the most liquid assets other assets those are relatively liquid and included in quick assets are debtors and bills receivable and marketable securities. As the inventories are treated as less liquid as they requires some time for

realizing into cash. The quick ratio is calculated as under:

Quick Ratio = Current Assets – Inventories Current Liabilities

Where…

Current Assets include cash and those assets which are convertible into cash within a period of one year.

Current Liabilities includes all obligations which are to maturing within a period of one year.

Inventories include all three types – Raw Material, Work In Process (WIP) and Finished Goods.

iii) Cash Ratio

Cash is considered to be the most liquid asset. The financial analysts normally examine cash ratio and its equivalent to current liabilities. Trade investment or marketable securities are equivalent of cash; therefore, they may be included in the computation of cash ratio.

The Cash ratio is calculated as under:

Cash Ratio = Cash + Marketable Securities Current Liabilities

Cash ratio can be more or less. The less ratio should also not to be the issue of huge concern as the company may have a strong reserve power.

iv) Interval Measure

The interval measure assesses the firm's ability to meet its regular cash expenses. The interval measure relates liquid assets to average daily operating cash outflows. The Interval Measure is calculated in number of days as under:

Interval Measure = Current Assets – Inventory
Average Daily Operating Expenses

Where…
Average Daily Operating Expenses =
[(Cost of Goods Sold + Selling & Admin overheads-Depreciation) / 360]

v) Net Working Capital Ratio

The difference between current assets and current liabilities (excluding short term bank borrowings) is known as Net Working Capital (NWC) *OR* Net Current Assets (NCA). NWC is sometimes used as a measure of a firm's liquidity. The ratio is calculated as under :

NWC Ratio = $\dfrac{\text{Net Working Capital (NWC)}}{\text{Net Assets.}}$

The NWC measuers the firm's potential reservoir of funds. It can be related to net assets (or Capital Employed)

All above ratios indicate firm's liquidity situation. But during the analysis it is to be considered that Current Assets & Current Liabilities keeps on changing at a rapid pace and can change quickly.

b) Leverage Ratios

Leverage Ratios are popularly known as the capital structure ratios as well. Any firm has got two sources of finance one is owned funds and the other is borrowed funds. As a general rule, there should be an appropriate mix of debt and owners' equity in financing the firm's assets. There are various implications of the manner in which the funds are arranged they can be prescribed as under:

1. The composition of debt and equity. The debt is considered as more risk from a firm's point of view. As it is obligation on the part of the firm to re-pay the amount along with the interest component.

2.The use of debt can also be sometimes advantageous in case where the firm can retain control of the firm with a limited stake and their earnings will be increased when a firm earns a rate which is higher than its cost of capital of borrowed funds.

3. It is observed that highly debt firm find it difficult to get appropriate return. As they are facing the problem of incremental level of marginal rate of interest

The process of magnifying the shareholders' return through use of debt is popularly known as 'trading on equity'. However, the situation can be different when the rates are reverse or the situation is different.

The leverage ratios are calculated on the basis of balance sheet, it may also be computed using profit and loss account by determining the extent to which operating profits are sufficient to cover the fixed charges.

i) Debt Ratio

The debt ratios can be considered to arrive at the ratio of proportion of total debt and net assets. The following two debt ratios are popular.

a)	Debt Ratio =	Total Debt
		Total Debt + Net Worth
	Where…	Total Debt + Net Worth = Capital Employed
b)	Debt Ratio =	Total Debt(TD)
		Net Assets(NA)

Where… Net Assets = Net Fixed Assets + Net Current Assets

It is to be noted that the Capital Employed (CE) equals Net Assets that consists of Net Fixed Assets (NFA) and Net Current Assets (NCA). The Net Current Assets are Current Assets (CA) minus Current Liabilities (CL) excluding interest bearing short term debt for working capital

ii) Debt – Equity Ratio

The Relationship describing the lenders' contribution for each rupee of the owners' contribution is called as debt-equity ratio. Debt-equity (DE) ratio is directly computed by dividing total debt by net worth.

Debt-Equity Ratio =	Total Debt
	Net Worth

The ratio can be less \ greater than 1 : 1 or equal to 1 : 1.

iii) Capital Employed to Net Worth Ratio

There is another way of expressing the basic relationship between debt and equity. One way can be How much funds are being contributed together by lenders and owners for each rupee of the owners' contribution? Calculating the ratio of capital employed or net assets to net worth can find this out :

CE-to-NW ratio = Capital Employed Net Worth

As the Capital Employed is normally equal to Net Assets, it can be replaced. Treatment of Preference share capital as debt ignores fact that debt and preference capital present different risk to shareholders. 6Heavy indebtedness leads to creditor's pressure on managements functioning.

iv) Interest Coverage Ratios

Debt ratios are described as a static in nature and many times make it difficult to exactly direct towards firm's ability to meet the interest or other fixed charges obligation.

The interest coverage ratio or the Times – interest-earned is used to test the firm's debt servicing capacity. The interest coverage ratio is calculated as under:

Interest Coverage =	EBIT
	Interest

Sometimes, the depreciation – being a non cash item it can be excluded. Therefore the interest coverage can also be computed as under :

Interest Coverage =	EBITDA
	Interest

This ratio indicates the extent to which earnings may fall without causing any embarrassment to the firm regarding the payment of the interest charges. A higher ratio is desirable; but too high a ratio indicates that the firm is very conservative in using debt and that it is not using credit to the best advantage of shareholders. A lower ratio indicates excessive use of debt or inefficient operations.

c) Activity Ratios

Activity Ratios are calculated evaluate the efficiency with which the firm manages and utilized its assets. These ratios are known as turnover ratios as well. The activity ratios involve a relationship between sales and assets. A proper balance between sales and assets generally reflects that assets are managed properly.

The following are the ratios that indicate level of activities.

i)Inventory Turnover Ratio

Inventory Turnover Ratio indicates the efficiency of the firm in manufacturing and selling of its product. The ratio is arrived at by Dividing cost of goods sold by the average inventory.

Inventory Turnover = $\frac{Cost\ Of\ Goods\ Sold}{Average\ Inventory}$

Where...

Average Inventory is the average of opening and closing balance of inventory.

When 360 (Appro. No. of days in a year) is divided by this ratio, it gives us days of inventory holding. Therefore,

Days of Inventory Holding =

The inventory turnover indicates how fast the inventory is turning into receivable through sales. Generally, a high level of inventory turnover indicates of good inventory management. For further analysis of inventory, this ratio may be divided into the following sub-ratios

a) Finished Goods Turnover

b) Work-in-process Turnover

c) Materials Turnover

d) Sales to total inventory

e) Inventory to Sales

ii) Debtors Turnover Ratio

When a firm sells goods on credit to its customers, debtors (Accounts receivables) are created in the firm's account. The debtors are convertible into cash over a short period and therefore, they are included in current assets. The liquidity position of the firm depends on the quality of debtors to a great extent. The debtors turnover ratio is calculated as under :

| Debtors Turnover = | Credit Sales |
| | Average Debtors |

The debtors turnover indicates the number of times debtors turnover each year. Generally, the higher the value of debtors turnover, more efficient is the management of credit.

When 360 (Approx no. of days in a year) is divided by this ratio, it gives us days of Collection Period. Therefore,

| Days of Collection Period = 360 Debtors Turnover |

The days of collection indicates the average number of days for which debtors remain outstanding. The interpretation of Average Collection Period should be done cautiously. It helps in determining collectability of debtors and ascertaining firm's collection experience.

iii) Assets Turnover Ratio and Working Capital Turnover

Assets are used to generate sales. Therefore, a firm is required to manage the assets with adequate efficiency to maximize sales. The relationship between Sales and Assets is known as Assets Turnover. There are several types of Assets Turnover can be calculated. But it is required to understand the following.

| NA = CE | |
| NA = NFA + (CA-CL) | or NA = NFA + NCA |

| TA = NFA + CA | |

Based on the above, there can be various types of Asset Turnover Ratio.

Net Asset Turnover =	Sales
	Net Assets
Total Asset Turnover =	Sales
	Total Assets
Fixed Asset Turnover =	Sales
	Net Fixed Assets
Net Current Assets Turnover =	Sales
	Net Current Assets
Current Assets Turnover =	Sales
	Current Assets

A firm's ability to produce a large volume of sales for a given amount of net asset is most important aspect of its operating performance. Unutilized or Under Utilized assets increase the firm's need for costly financing as well as expenses for maintenance and upkeep. The Asset Turnover Ratios should be interpreted cautiously.

d) Profitability Ratios

A majority of the discussion in the financial performance evolves around the concepts of profit maximization and wealth maximization. Profits are always essential. But it would not be appropriate to go ahead with the discussion of profit maximization until the concept of profit is properly understood. The method to arrive at profit is as under:

	Sales / Total Income
Less	Cost of Goods Sold
	PBITDA
Less	Interest

	PBDTA
Less	Depreciation
	PBT
Less	Tax & Adjustments
	PAT
Add	Depreciation & Non Cash Exp
	Cash Profit.

Where…	
PBITDA =	Profit Before Interest Tax Depreciation & Adjustments
PBDTA =	Profit Before Depreciation Tax & Adjustments
PBDTA =	Profit Before Depreciation Tax & Adjustments
PBT =	Profit Before Tax
PAT =	Profit After Tax

Cash Profit = Profit After Tax + Depreciation (and other non cash exps.)

A firm's performance is often judged by the profitability. However, two types of profitability ratios are calculated.

a) Profitability in relation to sales.
b) Profitability in relation to investments.

The following are the ratios that profitability position of a firm. It is a fact that sufficient profit must be earned by a firm to sustain, expand and grow.

i) Gross Profit Margin

Gross profit is the first profitability ratio. It is calculated on gross Profitability margin, It is calculated as under:

Gross Profit Margin = Sales – Cost of Goods Sold Sales
=Gross Profit Sales

The gross profit margin reflects the efficiency with which management produces each unit of product. This ratio also indicates the aggregate spread between the Cost of Goods Sold (COGS) and the sales revenue. A high gross profit margin ratio can be sign of good management. The high gross margin may be due to any of the following

a) Higher sales prices, while cost of goods sold remain constant.
b) Lower Cost of Goods Sold, sales pricing remaining constant.
c) An increase in the proportionate volume of higher margin items.

The analysis of these factors will reveal to the management how a depressed gross profit margin can be improved.

A lower gross profit margin may reflect higher cost of goods sold due to the firm's inability to purchase raw materials at favorable terms, and inefficient utilization of plant and machinery or over investment in plant and machinery, resulting in higher cost of production.

ii) Net Profit Margin

Net profit is obtained by deducting operating expenses, interest and taxes are subtracted from the gross profit. The net profit margin ratio is measured by dividing profit after tax by sales. The formula can be narrated as under:

Net Profit Margin = Profit After Tax
                    Sales

Net profit margin ratio establishes relationship between net profit and sales. It also indicates management's efficiency in manufacturing, administering and selling the products. This ratio is overall measure of the firm's ability to turn each rupee sales into net profit. If the net margin is inadequate, the firm will fail to achieve satisfactory return on shareholders' funds.

iii) Operating Expense Ratio

Where a firm with higher net margin ratio will be in advantageous, position to survive in the face of falling selling prices, rising costs of production or declining demand for the product Such conditions are very difficult for low profit margin firms.

The operating expense ratio explains the changes in the profit margin. (EBIT to Sales) ratio, This ratio is computed by dividing operating expenses *viz.* cost of goods sold plus selling expenses and general and administrative expenses (excluding interest) by sales:

Operating Expense Ratio = Operating Expenses Sales

A higher operating expense ratio is un-favourable as it indicates a smaller amount of operating income to meet interest, dividends etc. The variations in this ratio can be because of various reasons like:

a) Changes in Sales Prices
b) Changes in the demand for the product

c)	Changes in administrative or selling expenses	or
d)	Changes in the proportionate shares of sales	of different products

with varying gross margins.

These, along with other causes are reasons for variations in the ratio.

iv) Return on Investment

Term investment is equal to 'Total Assets' or 'Net Assets'. The funds employed in net assets are known as capital employed. Net Assets is equal to Net Fixed Assets plus Current Assets minus Current Liabilities (Excluding Bank Loans). Alternatively, capital employed is equal to net worth plus total debt.

As per the conventional approach of calculating Return on Investment (ROI) is to divide PAT by investment, Investment indicates pool of funds supplied by shareholders and lenders.

The taxes are not something which is within the control of management, and since the firm's opportunities for availing tax incentives differ, it is more prudent to use before-tax measure of ROI. The following two methods indicate calculation of ROI.

ROI =	ROTA =	$\dfrac{EBIT}{TA}$
ROI =	RONA =	$\dfrac{EBIT}{NA}$

Some companies even use EBITDA to calculate the ROI.

v) Return on Equity

The common shareholder is entitled to the residual profits. A return on shareholders' equity is calculated to see the profitability of owners' investment. The shareholders' equity or net worth will include paid-up share capital, share premium and reserves and surplus less accumulated losses. Net worth can also by found by subtracting total liabilities from total assets.

The return on equity is net profit after taxes divided by shareholders' equity which is given by net worth.

ROE =	Profit After Taxes = Net Worth (Equity)	$\dfrac{PAT}{NW}$

ROE indicates how well the firm has used the resources of owners. The earning of a satisfactory return is the most desirable objective of a business. The ratio of net profit to owners' equity reflects the extent to which this objective is accomplished.

Therefore, this ratio is great interest to the present as well as the prospective shareholders and also great concern to management.

The return on owners' equity of the company is normally compared with the ratios for other similar companies and the industry average. This reveals the relative performance and strength of the company in attracting future investments.

vi) Earnings Per Share

The Earnings Per Share is one of the key measure of profitability of shareholders' investment. The EPS is calculated by dividing the profit after taxes by total number of ordinary shares outstanding. The formulae to calculate EPS is as under :

EPS =	Profit After Tax
	Number of Outstanding Shares

The calculation of EPS over the years indicates whether the firm's earnings power on per-share basis has changed over that period or not. The EPS of the Company should be compared with industry average and the EPS of the other firms. However, EPS does not indicate how much of EPS is distributed as a dividend and how much is retained earnings.

vii) Dividend Per Share

The dividend is the income which a shareholder really receives. This is the amount which is a part of earnings distributed as cash to the shareholders. Therefore, it is a large number of interest to majority of the investors. Some investors put greater weightage on Dividend Per Share rather than on EPS.

The DPS is calculated as under:

DPS = Earnings paid to shareholders (Dividends)/Number of ordinary shares outstanding

Now, for example a company earns Rs. 8.00 per share and distributes Rs. 2.00 per share, then the difference per share is retained in the business.

viii) Dividend Payout Ratio

The dividend payout ratio is the comparison of amount distributed as dividend and amount earned per share. The payout ratio is calculated as under.

Payout Ratio =	Dividend Per Share
	Earnings Per Share

Earnings not distributed per share are retained in the business. Therefore, retention ratio in the business will be equal to 1 – Payout Ratio. If this figure is multiplied by ROE, one can know the growth in the owners' equity as a result of retention policy.

ix) Dividend and Earnings Yield

The dividend yield is the dividends per share divided by market value per share. It can be calculated as under :

Dividend Yield =	Dividend Per Share =	DPS
	Market Value Per Share	MV

The earnings yield is the earnings per share divided by market value per share. It can be calculated as under:

Earnings Yield =	Earnings Per Share	= EPS
	Market Value Per Share	MV

Above ratios evaluate the shareholders' return in relation to the market value of the share. The earnings yield ratio is also called as Earnings – Price (E/P) Ratio.

x) Price Earnings Ratio

This ratio is reciprocal to the above ratio. This is one of the most popular among the financial analysts to value the firm's performance as expected by the shareholders. This can be calculated as under :

P/E Ratio	=	Market Value Per Share	= MV
		Earnings Per Share	EPS

This also indicates investors' judgment or expectations about the firm's performance.

Normally, this ratio reflects investors' expectations about the growth in the firm's earnings.

xi) Market Value to Book Value Ratio

This ratio is primarily indication of market v/s book value of share. Hence, it is the ratio of share price to book value per share :

M/B Ratio	=	Market Value Per Share
		Book Value Per Share

Where...

Book Value Per Share = Net Worth
   No. of shares outstanding

This is also an indication of the company's worth compared to funds which are put into by shareholders.

II. FINANCIAL STATEMENT ANALYSIS

1) COMPARATIVE STATEMENT ANALYSIS

Comparative Statement Analysis is one of the methods to trace periodic change in the financial performance of a firm.

The changes over the period are described by way of Increase of Decrease in income statement and balance sheet. The changes are normally of two types :
i) Aggregate Changes
ii) Proportional Change

A sample of comparative statement is described as under:

Particulars	Previous Year (Amt. Rs.)	Current Year (Amt. Rs.)	Change (in Amt)	Change (in %)
Liabilities and Capital				
Current Liabilities	XX	XX	(+ / -)	(+ / -) %
Long Term Liabilities	XX	XX	(+ / -)	(+ / -) %
Share Capital & Res.	XX	XX	(+ / -)	(+ / -) %
Total	XX	XX	(+ / -)	(+ / -) %
Assets	-			
Fixed Assets	XX	XX	(+ / -)	(+ / -) %
Current Assets	XX	XX	(+ / -)	(+ / -) %
Other Assets	XX	XX	(+ / -)	(+ / -) %
Total	XX	XX	(+ / -)	(+ / -)

The financial statement mentioned in above table indicates corresponding changes in two balance sheet data. An assessment of comparative financial statement helps to highlight the significant facts and points out the items requiring further analysis. All annual report of the selected companies provides data related to last two financial years.

2) COMMMON SIZE STATEMENT ANALYSIS

A common size financial statement displays all items as percentages of a common base figure rather than as absolute numerical figures. This type of financial statement allows for easy analysis between companies or between time periods for the same company. The values on the common size statement are expressed as ratios or percentages of a statement component, such as revenue.

While most firms don't report their statements in common size format, it is beneficial for analysts to compute it to compare two or more companies of differing size or different sectors of the economy. Formatting financial statements in this way reduces bias that can occur and allows for the analysis of a company over various time periods, revealing, for example, what percentage of sales is the cost of goods sold and how that value has changed over time. Common size financial statements commonly include the income statement, balance sheet and cash flow statement.

❖ COMMON SIZE INCOME STATEMENT

The income statement, also referred to as the profit and loss (P&L) statement, provides an overview of flows of sales, expenses and net income during the reporting period. The income statement equation is sales minus expenses and adjustments equals net income. This is why the common size income statement defines all items as a percentage of sales. The term "common size" is most often used when analyzing elements of the income statement, but the balance sheet and the cash flow statement can also be expressed as a common size statement.

For example, if a company has a simple of income statement with gross sales = $100,000, cost of goods sold = $50,000, taxes = $1,000 and net income = $49,000, the common size statement would read:

Sales	1.00
Cost of goods sold	0.50
Taxes	0.01
Net Income	0.49

Common Size Balance Sheet Statement

The balance sheet provides a snapshot overview of the firm's assets, liabilities and shareholders' equity for the reporting period. A common size balance sheet is set up with the same logic as the common size income statement. The balance sheet equation is assets equals liabilities plus stockholders' equity. As a result, analysts define the balance sheet as a percentage of assets. Another version of the common size balance sheet shows asset line items as a percentage of total assets, liabilities as a percentage of total liabilities and stockholders' equity as a percentage of total stockholders' equity.

3). TREND ANALYSIS

This is a very easy way to evaluate the performance of a firm. In this, the current year's financial ratios are compared over a period of time. This is an indication of direction of the firm's direction of change..

Here, the role of analyst is also becoming important. It should be noted that the analyst should not only stick to mathematical aspect of the ratio. They should go into root cause and try to analyze the reasons behind changing trend of ratios.

❖ Cross Sectional Analysis \ Inter-firm analysis

When the financial ratio of one firm is compared with some selected firms in the same industry, at the same point of time, it is known as Cross Sectional Analysis or Inter-firm analysis.

In many cases, comparison of firm's performance with carefully selected firms from the industry is more beneficial. It may indicate the firm's strengths or weaknesses in terms of operating leverage or financial leverage.

The Time Series Analysis or Trend Analysis indicates of ratio indicates the direction of changes. The trend analysis is advocated to be studied in light of the following two factors.

i)The rate of fixed expansion or secular trend in the growth of the business and

ii) The general price level.

Any increase sales statement may be because of two reasons, one may be the increase in volume of business and another is the variation in prices of the goods / services.

For trend analysis, the use of index number is generally advocated. The procedure followed is to assign the number 100 to the items of each base year and to calculate percentage changes in each item of the other years in relation to the base year. This is known as 'Trend-Percentage Method'. The following table indicates it.

Particulars	Base Year	Previous Year	Current Year
Sales	100		
EBIT	100	(+ / -)	(+ / -)
PAT	100	(+ / -)	(+ / -)
Current Assets	100	(+ / -)	(+ / -)
Current Liabilities	100	(+ / -)	(+ / -)
Gross Fixed Assets	100	(+ / -)	(+ / -)
Net Assets	100	(+ / -)	(+ / -)
Total Assets	100	(+ / -)	(+ / -)
Net Worth	100	(+ / -)	(+ / -)
Dividend	100	**(+ / -)**	**(+ / -)**

III. DuPont Analysis

According to the Du-Pont analysis, RONA (or ROCE) is an important tool for judging the operating financial performance 4. It is an indication of the earning power of the firm.

	RONA is calculated as under :				
RONA =	EBIT NA =	Sales X NA	GP X Sales	EBIT GP	
Where : RONA =	Return on Net Assets				
EBIT	Earnings Before Interest and				

	=	Tax
GP		Gross Profit
	=	
NA		Net Assets
	=	

It is observed that most of the firms would like to improve their RONA. However, in this competitive world, RONA is always under pressure. Hence, firms have to balance between the Asset Turnover and Gross profit Margin. Many firms adopt various ways to increase the Gross Profit Margin some firms resort to vertical integration for cost reduction also.

A firm can convert impressive RONA into an impressive ROE through financial efficiency. It is observed that ROE us certainly affected by the Financial leverage and combination of debt and equity. Therefore, ROE is a product of RONA and financial leverage ratios which reflect the operating efficiency.

Therefore, ROE = Operating Performance X	Leverage Factor.

The Du-pont chart can also be indicated with the help of the following diagramme.
Return on Equity

Return on Net Assets	Financial Leverage (Bal. Sheet)	Financial Leverage (Income)

Profit Margin Assets Turnover

Therefore, the combined effect of the du-pont chart can be explained with the following.

ROE = Sales x	GP x	EBIT x	PAT x	NA
NA	Sales	GP	EBIT	NW

As discussed above, ROE when it is multiplied by retention ratio gives growth.

(B) MOREDEN TOOLS COVERS
1) EVA (ECONOMICAL VALUE ADDED)

Many companies are now linking major financial decisions to Economic Value Added, or EVA. Essentially, this is net operating profit on an after-tax basis minus a charge for the opportunity cost of capital.

1. It gives a one-period addition to value from a company's operations.
2. Using EVA allows the financial manager to integrate short-term decisions having both revenues and costs into the company's capital budgeting process, for those companies not using NPV or which prefer to merge all decisions into one decision-making framework.

❖ The following formula gives the formula for calculating EVA, followed by an illustrative example.

EVA = Operating Profit After Tax − (Cost of Capital)(Capital Employed)

Illustrative Example:

Dwenger & Associates, a medical care practice, has a weighted-average cost of capital of 10%. It has employed $30,000,000 of mostly long-term capital to run the practice, according to the most recent balance sheet. The most recent income statement shows the following:

Revenues	$40,000,000
- COGS	24,000,000
Gross profit	16,000,000
- Operating expenses	7,500,000
After-tax Operating profit:	$ 8,500,000
	− 40% tax on this profit ($3,400,000)
	$5,100,000

The Economic Value Added for this period would be $2,100,000, calculated as follows:

$$\begin{aligned} EVA &= \text{Operating Profit After Tax} \\ &\quad - (\text{Cost of Capital})(\text{Capital Employed}) \\ &= \$5{,}100{,}000 - (0.10)(\$30{,}000{,}000) = \underline{\mathbf{\$2{,}100{,}000}} \end{aligned}$$

2) BALANCE SCORE CARD
Objectives, Measures, Targets, and Initiatives

Within each of the Balanced Scorecard financial, customer, internal process, and learning perspectives, the firm must define the following:

- **Strategic objectives** - what the strategy is to achieve in that perspective.
- **Measures** - how progress for that particular objective will be measured.
- **Targets** - the target value sought for each measure.
- **Initiatives** - what will be done to facilitate the reaching of the target?

The following sections provide examples of some objectives and measures for the four perspectives.

❖ Financial Perspective

The financial perspective addresses the question of how shareholders view the firm and which financial goals are desired from the shareholder's perspective. The specific goals depend on the company's stage in the business life cycle.

For example:

- **Growth stage** - goal is growth, such as revenue growth rate
- **Sustain stage** - goal is profitability, such ROE, ROCE, and EVA
- **Harvest stage** - goal is cash flow and reduction in capital requirements

The following table outlines some examples of financial metrics:

Objective	Specific Measure
Growth	Revenue growth
Profitability	Return on equity
Cost leadership	Unit cost

❖ **Customer Perspective**

The customer perspective addresses the question of how the firm is viewed by its customers and how well the firm is serving its targeted customers in order to meet the financial objectives. Generally, customers view the firm in terms of time, quality, performance, and cost. Most customer objectives fall into one of those four categories. The following table outlines some examples of specific customer objectives and measures:

Objective	Specific Measure
New products	% of sales from new products
Responsive supply	On time delivery
To be preferred supplier	Share of key accounts
Customer partnerships	Number of cooperative efforts

❖ **Internal Process Perspective**

Internal business process objectives address the question of which processes are most critical for satisfying customers and shareholders. These are the processes in which the firm must concentrate its efforts to excel. The following table outlines some examples of process objectives and measures:

Objective	Specific Measure
Manufacturing excellence	Cycle time, yield
Increase design productivity	Engineering efficiency
Reduce product launch delays	Actual launch date vs. plan

❖ Learning and Growth Perspective

Learning and growth metrics address the question of how the firm must learn, improve, and innovate in order to meet its objectives. Much of this perspective is employee-centered. The following table outlines some examples of learning and growth measures:

Objective	Specific Measure
Manufacturing learning	Time to new process maturity
Product focus	% of products representing 80% of sales
Time to market	Time compared to that of competitors

❖ References

1. Pandey I M (2005) *Ninth Edition Financial Management* PP 517 – 544
2. Foster G, *Financial Statement Analysis*, Prentice Hall 1986 pp 2-7
3. Anthony, R N and Reece, J S , *Management Accounting Principles,* Taraporewala, 1975 pp 260-263
4. Foster G, *Financial Statement Analysis*, Prentice Hall 1986
5. Barges, Alexander, *The effect of Capital structure on the cost of capital,* Prentice-Hall inc. 1963, p 35.
6. Miller D E, *The meaningful interpretation of financial statement*, AMA 1966 Miller Op. Cit P 67.
7. Drucker, P.F., *The Practice of Management*, Pan 1968, pp 99-100.
8. Kennedy, R D and Mc Muller, *S. Y. Financial Statement* , Richard D Irwin p 404.
9. Brealey R and Myers S, *Principles of Corporate Finance*, McGraw Hill, 1984 p. 578.

CHAPTER : 3

RESEARCH METHODOLOGY

INDEX

SR.NO.	CONTENTS	PAGE NO
3.1	INTRODUCTION	81
3.2	WHY RESEARCH	82
3.3	RESEARCH DEFINITION	83
3.4	INTRODUCTION ABOUT TRADING HOUSES IN INDIA	83
3.5	IDENTIFICATION AND GAP ANALYSIS	84
3.6	REVIEW OF LITERATURE	85
3.7	STATEMENT OF THE PROBLEM	95
3.8	OBJECTIVES OF THE STUDY	96
3.9	HYPOTHESIS OF THE STUDY	96
3.10	UNIVERSE OF THE STUDY	97
3.11	SAMPLE OF THE STUDY	98
3.12	SAMPLING TECHNIQUE	98
3.13	DATA ANALYSIS	98
3.14	TOOLS AND TECHNIQUES	98
3.15	LIMITATIONS OF THE STUDY	98
3.16	SIGNIFICANTS OF THE STUDY	98
3.17	OUTLINE OF THE THESIS	99
3.18	SCOPE OF THE STUDY	100
❖	REFERENCES	102

3.1. INTRODUCTION

One of the essential keys to any research work is the research and analysis of its steps that are implemented in the society. These steps must be suitable to test hypotheses of the research and also to help the access capability of overall design of the research such as collection of data and analysis of data. This chapter describes the approaches that are used in this study in order to test the hypotheses of the problem under the study and provides the reader with a basis for calculating the validity of findings, an understanding of the basis for choices that were made and sufficient details that another researcher can replicate this study. In this chapter, some vital objects related to research methodology such as problem under the study, initial literature review, objectives and hypotheses and their methodologies developed for them, data instruments including collection of data and analysis of data are in details explained and finally at the end of this chapter the limitations and conclusion of research methodology are stated.

The study conducted followed a survey method. The design produces the picture of the phenomenon in which the decision maker is interested. Since only small amount of secondary data was available on the subject, the research focused on collection and analysis of primary data. Survey method was adopted to collect the primary data.

Research design specifies the methods and procedures for collection of requisite information and its measurements and analysis to arrive at certain meaningful conclusion at the end of the proposed study. Researchers conducted this research with the help of Questionnaire and from the initial stages, to the final designing of questionnaire; they conducted their research through exploratory research as well as Descriptive research.

3.2 WHY RESEARCH?

I have referred so many articles and journals about trading houses and also having a keen interest in the field of research what happened in the trading houses and what are the element and processes of trading and trading agencies so I have decided to take initiative to do research on this particular topic. I have selected 30 top trading houses to analysed research to find out various ratios like profitability, current, cash, inventory, working capital etc.

Research is concerned with increasing our understanding. Research provides us with the information and knowledge needed for problem solving and making decisions. Researcher's focus here is applied research for decision making for public policy. In this context the purpose of research is problem solving technique prescription of problem and the solutions of the problem. As here researcher have keen interest to understand trading houses, to know about financial ratios, to analysed financial ratio, profitability ratio, working capital ratio, to analysed asset ratio of the selected samples and to provide valuable suggestions to the world and to researchers who will further conduct research on that particular area of research.

Problem solving can be broken down into a number of separate components, each of which requires information and analysis of following.

- identification of problems
- diagnosis of causes
- identification of potential solutions
- decision for action
- monitoring and evaluation of action and outcomes

Information for policy making will therefore serve or more of the following functions.

- Description - to provide baseline data or simply a picture of how things are.
- Explanation (analytical) - to understand why things are the way they are, what factors explain the way things are.
- Prediction - to predict how systems will change under alternative scenarios (modeling).
- Prescription and planning (decision-making) - prescription and planning relating to changes in existing systems.
- Monitoring and evaluation - monitoring and evaluation of the effects of changes during and after they have been made. Investigations may be made to compare

results in practice with predictions, or to monitor the effects of a policy, management technique or treatment.

3.3. RESEARCH DEFINITION

According to **Greenfield (1996)** defines that the research is an original contribution to the existing stock of knowledge making for its development. The systematic approach concerning generalizations and formulation of a theory is also research. As such the term „research" refers to the systematic method consisting of enunciating the problem, formulating a hypothesis, collecting the data, analyzing the facts and reaching certain conclusions either in the form of solutions(s) towards the concerned problem or in certain generation for some theoretical formulation.

Research is an art aided by skills of inquiry, experimental design, data collection, measurement and analysis, by interpretation, and by presentation. A further skill, which can be acquired and developed, is creativity or invention.

Noltingk (1965) believes that Research is in essence an investigation into processes. Therefore a research is the finding of answers related to the questions. It is a systematic search for truth, finding new knowledge about our world through combination of ideas and facts.

3.4 INTRODUCTION ABOUT TRADING HOUSES IN INDIA

Trading Houses are of various types and forms. They exist in a number of countries and their activities and organization vary according to the historical background and the scenario in which they operate as well as national priorities and government policies. They are known by different names in different countries. So it is difficult to formulate a definition of Trading Houses which would be universally applicable. There are, however, resemblances in certain important aspects in the organizational structures of most of Trading Houses which make it possible for them to be analyzed as one generic entity. It is thus possible to describe activities, organization and definition of Trading Houses which would be universally applicable.

A definition that covers most cases is "Trading Houses are commercial intermediaries specialized in the long term development of trade in goods & services supplied by the other parties" they focus on exporting, importing and third country trading as their core activity and use overseas marketing organization and infrastructure as well as procurement networks to service suppliers and customers. They procure internationally and sell locally and they also procure internationally and sell internationally. They have flexibility and the agility to work in many markets with many products simultaneously as international marketing is their core business. They serve as commercial intermediaries between suppliers and buyers located in different countries.

Government of India has a scheme to recognize established exporters as Exports Houses, Trading House etc. Trading Houses are special category of exporters which enjoy export incentives granted by Government on exporting of goods & services.

A Trading House is defined as a registered exporter holding a valid and special category of export house certificate issued by the DGFT.

3.5 IDENTIFICATION AND GAP ANALYSIS

Since the world grows smaller, companies should continue to reach across borders provided they wish to compete successfully in today's international economy. Domestic markets have been saturating in many countries resulting in slumps. Still companies with the vision to cross barrier and trade to global market will watch profits soar.

From the beginning of the second five year plan, the foreign exchange problem began to assume serious proportion, and the government began to realize the need for vigorous export promotion. It was very clear that concentrated efforts should be made for the promotion of export of non-traditional items. It was also realized that unless positive steps were taken to build up a number of merchant houses, concentrating almost exclusively on exports and capable of undertaking trade on a sustained basis, it would be impossible to compete successfully against the highly experienced and resourceful trading houses of others countries.

The present study deals with the aspect of Financial Performance Analyses of Trading Houses in India. The Main aim of study is to analyze Financial Performance of selected companies working as Trading Houses mainly related with exports and imports of goods and services. Export sector is most dynamic sector with the advantages such as (1) Earning of Foreign Exchange (2) Employment Generation (3)

Exports allow fuller utilization of capacity (4) Increased Exports has been strongly associated with the reduction of poverty in most developing countries and (5) overall development of the country.

The major challenges faced by the financial manager are to see that there is sufficient liquidity to pay back current liabilities without blocking too much funds. We know that firm"s aim at maximizing the wealth of shareholders. The financial manager should determine the optimum level of current assets so that the wealth of shareholders is maximized.

3.6 REVIEW OF LETRATURE

1. **AUTHOR NAME -**: Nizam Mohammed
2. **YEAR- :**1985
3. **REVIEW -:**

In his study entitled "Indian Paper Industry: Heading for a Bright Future" has analyzed the causes of low capacity utilization during the 1970s. He observes that the major problem which causes the relatively low capacity utilization include the shortage of raw materials, inadequate supply of power, coal and transport bottlenecks. He has also observed that the capacity utilization in paper industry is influenced by several factors.

1. **AUTHOR NAME -**: Ramanchandran and Janakiraman
2. **YEAR- :**2009
3. **REVIEW -:**

Analyzed the relationship between working capital management efficiency and earnings before interest and tax of the paper industries in India The study revealed that cash conversion cycle and inventory days had negative correlation with earnings before interest and tax. While accounts payable days and accounts receivable days related positively with earnings before interest and tax.

1. AUTHOR NAME -: Burange & et al.

2. YEAR- : 2008

3. REVIEW -:

    Deals with the "Performance of Indian Cement Industry - The Competitive Landscape" The Cement Industry is experiencing a boom on account of the overall growth of the Indian Economy primarily because of increased industrial activity, and expanding investment in the cement sector. The industry experienced a complete shift in the technology of production. The competitiveness among the firms in Indian Cement Industry has also been evaluated for the year 2006-2007, out of seventeen firms (90.21 per cent of the total market share), about 47 per cent have been recorded, above industry average performance in the overall competitiveness index.

1. AUTHOR NAME -: Adolphus

2. YEAR- : 2008

3. REVIEW -:

    Showed that there was a statistically significant relationship between measure of liquidity and selected measures of profitability, efficiency and indebtedness in Nigerian quoted manufacturing companies. The impact of one per cent increase in average liquidity measures produces a more significant increase in average profitability (21.9 per cent), efficiency (16.1 per cent) and indebtedness (16.6 per cent).

1. AUTHOR NAME -: Krishnaveni

2. YEAR- : 2007

3. REVIEW -:

    Studied the performance appraisal might be said that the adoption of liberalization measure and above suggestions would doubtlessly help the Indian chemical industry to improve their performance individually and other industry as a whole. This study also suggests that the policy of liberalization should further be strengthened. Thus, the dreams of our planners to accelerate the economic growth in the country are still possible to be translated into reality

1. AUTHOR NAME -: Vishnani and Shah

2. YEAR- : 2007

3. REVIEW -:

Investigated the impact of working capital management policies on the corporate performance of the India consumer electronics industry They noted that inventory holding period, debtors" collection period and net working capital cycle had negative relationship on the profitability of firms. Whereas, the average payment periods positive correlation with profitability.

1. AUTHOR NAME -: Sudarsana Reddy & et al.
2. YEAR- : 2006
3. REVIEW -:

Examined the internal funds availability for financing fixed assets in paper industry in Andhra Pradesh, The study found that the owner funds were insufficient to finance fixed assets and observed that fixed assets did not have significant relationship with the sales.

1. AUTHOR NAME -: Ooghe & et al.
2. YEAR- : 2006
3. REVIEW -:

In their paper examine the financial performance of the acquiring firm after the acquisition, using statistical analysis of industry- adjusted variables. Their findings show that following: the acquisition, the profitability, the solvency and the liquidity of most of the combined companies decline. This decline is also reflected in the failure prediction scores. With respect to the added value, acquisitions are found to be accompanied by increases in the labour productivity, but this is caused by the general improvement of gross added value per employee of Belgian companies in the last ten years. So, it seems that, contrary to the general expectations and beliefs, acquisitions usually do not seem to improve the acquirer's financial performance.

1. AUTHOR NAME -: Alovsat Muslumov

2. YEAR- :2005

3. REVIEW -:

"The Financial and Operating Performance of Privatization Companies in Turkish Cement Industry" This paper examines the post- privatization performance of privatized companies in the Turkish cement industry. The findings indicate that, when performance criteria for both the state and private enterprises are considered, privatization in the cement industry results in significant performance deterioration. Total value added and the return on investment declines significant after privatization. This decrease mainly stems from deterioration in asset productivity. The decline in asset productivity, however, is not caused by an increase in capital investment, since post- privatization capital investment did not change significantly. Significant contraction in total employment and an increase in financial leverage after privatization are among the key research findings. Privatization through public offering, gradual privatization and domestic ownership are found to stimulate the financial and operating performance of firms.

1. AUTHOR NAME -: Sukudev Singh & et al.

2. YEAR- : 2003

3. REVIEW -:

Undertook a study entitled "Status and Growth of Paper and Pulp Board Industry in North India – A Case study". The study has revealed that due to the availability of raw materials and labour, eighty per cent of the mills are running with the optimum capacity utilization. The authors have observed that more than three thousand people have got employment in ten paper and paper board mills with proportion of thousand eight hundred skilled workers and thousand two hundred unskilled labours. The authors have found out that the major problem faced by the industry is frequent breakdown of paper production especially during the summer season due to scarcity of power supply.

1. AUTHOR NAME -: Sudarsana Reddy

2. YEAR- : 2003

3. REVIEW -:

Under took a study on "Financial Performance of Paper Industry in Andhra Pradesh" for the period from 1989-90 to 1998-99. The primary objective of the study was to analyze the investment pattern and utilization of fixed assets, ascertaining the working capital condition, reviewing the profitability performance and suggesting measures to improve the profitability. He concluded that the introduction of additional funds along with restructuring of finances and modernization of technology were needed for better operating performance.

1. AUTHOR NAME -: Anshan Lakshmi

2. YEAR- : 2003

3. REVIEW -:

Made "A Study of the Financial Performance with Reference to Steel Industries Kerala Ltd". This study covered from 1977-1998 to 2001-2002. The objectives of the study was to analyze and evaluate the working capital management, to analyze the liquidity position of the company, to evaluate the receivables, payables and cash management and to suggest ways and means to improve the present date of working capital. The major tools used for the analysis said that the working capital management suggested that the inventory management have to be corrected

1. AUTHOR NAME -: Feroz & et al.

2. YEAR- : 2003

3. REVIEW -:

Ratio analysis is a commonly used analytical tool for verifying the performance of a firm. While ratios are easy to compute, which in part explains their wide appeal, their interpretation is problematic, especially when two or more ratios provide conflicting signals. Indeed, ratio analysis is often criticized on the grounds of subjectivity that is the analyst must pick and choose ratios in order to assess the overall performance of a firm. In this paper they demonstrate that Data Envelopment Analysis (DEA) can augment the traditional ratio analysis. DEA can provide a consistent and reliable measure of managerial or operational efficiency of a firm. They test the null hypothesis that there is no relationship between DEA and traditional accounting ratios as measures of performance of a firm. Their results reject the null hypothesis indicating that DEA can provide information to analysts that is additional to that provided by traditional ratio analysis. They also apply DEA to the oil and gas industry to demonstrate.

1. AUTHOR NAME -: sahu
2. YEAR- : 2002
3. REVIEW -:

in his article titled "A Simplified Model for Liquidity Analysis of Paper Industry" has examined the liquidity of paper industry. The model developed by him has been based on the assumption that the liquidity management of a company in a particular year is effective if its" earnings before depreciation is positive and not effective if its" earnings before depreciation is negative. The findings have revealed a very high predictive ability of the estimated discriminate function.

1. AUTHOR NAME -: Bortolotti & et al.
2. YEAR- : 2002
3. REVIEW -:

Examine the financial and operating performance of thirty one national telecommunication companies in twenty five countries that were fully or partially privatized through public share offering. Using conventional pre-versus post-privatization comparisons and panel data estimation techniques, they find that the financial and operating performance of telecommunications companies improves significantly after privatization, but that a sizable fraction of the observed improvement results from regulatory changes-alone or in combination with major ownership changes-rather than from privatization alone.

1. AUTHOR NAME -: Mahes Chand Garg and Chander Shekhar
2. YEAR- : 2002
3. REVIEW -:

Found that the asset composition is to be significantly negatively related with total Debt equity and long term dept equity in cement industries. Value of the assets and life of the company were significantly positively related to total debt equity. Life of the company was significantly positively related with long term debt equity in cement industries. The regression coefficient of collateral value of assets was significant at 10 per cent level and was positively associated with total debt equity.

1. AUTHOR NAME -: Harris
2. YEAR- : 2001
3. REVIEW -:

Analyses the link between market orientation and performance has been claimed largely on the basis of the analysis of subjective measures of performance. Consequently, the aim of this study is to examine the links between market orientation and objectively measured financial performance. The paper begins with a brief examination of the definition and components of market orientation. Thereafter, extant research into the consequences of developing market orientation is reviewed critically, leading to the development of a number of research hypotheses. After detailing the research design and methodology adopted in this study, the findings of a survey of UK industry are presented. Briefly, the results indicate that when subjective measures of performance are adopted, market orientation is associated with company performance in certain environmental conditions. However, when objective measures of performance are adopted, there is a narrower range of environmental conditions where market orientation is positively associated with performance. The paper concludes with a series of implications for both theorists and practitioners.

1. AUTHOR NAME -: Muhammad Rafiqul Islam
2. YEAR- : 2000
3. REVIEW -:

"Working Capital Management of Paper Mills in Bangladesh-An Overall View" concluded that all the units of the paper industry had failed to manage their working capital requirements properly. The reasons for working capital crisis were improper use of short-term funds, operating losses, over stocking to stores and spares; and non-availability of raw- materials.

1. AUTHOR NAME -: Gangadhar

2. YEAR- : 1998

3. REVIEW -:

has made an attempt on "Financial Analysis of Companies in Criteria: A Profitability and efficiency focus" one of the objectives of the study is to analyze the liquidity position of the companies and to point out the factors responsible for such a position. It is concluded that the liquidity position was quite alarming since these are facing chronic liquidity problems. Their proportion current assets in relation to the current liabilities are very low. It is suggested that, they may be improved by reducing excessive burden of current liabilities or increasing the level of current assets depending upon the requirements.

1. AUTHOR NAME -: Roger M. Shelor & et al.

2. YEAR- : 1998

3. REVIEW -:

This study examines changes in "Operating Performance among Real Estate Investment Trusts" following an Initial Public Offering (IPO). The purpose is to determine whether there is an enhancement in the value of the underlying asset that is related to the IPO. They analyze equity, mortgage and diversified REITs separately. They also compare the operating performance of recent IPOs to those of earlier years to address the impact of the 1993 Revenue Reconciliation Act on institutional investors" demand for REIT stock. Unlike previous analyses of industrial firms, REITs were found to have significant increases in return on Assets and selected measures of financial performance. The post-IPO cumulative stock price decline and recovery is illustrated.

1. AUTHOR NAME -: Sukamal Datta

2. YEAR- : 1995

3. REVIEW -:

In his study entitled "Working Capital Management through Financial Statements: Analysis of Paper Industry in West Bengal" found that most of the firms were suffering from shortage of working capital. One of the primary causes of such shortage of working capital was that most of the firms under study were not capable of earning adequate profit and were also suffering from losses. The expansion of fixed asserts also caused the working capital crisis. The utilization of fund had not been covered by sufficient amount of fund by way of long-term investment.

1. **AUTHOR NAME** -: Srinivasa Rao and Indrasena Reddy
2. **YEAR-** : 1995
3. **REVIEW -:**

In their study entitled "Financial Performance in Paper Industry- A Case Study" stated that the financial position of the company had been improving from year to year. The company"s performance in relation to generating internal funds in the form of reserves and surplus was excellent and also was doing well in mobilizing outside funds. The liquidity position of the company was sound as it was revealed by current and liquid ratios which were above the standard. The solvency ratios showed that the company had been following the policy of low capital gearing from 1990-91 as these ratios had been decreasing from this year. The performance of the company in relation to its profitability was not up to the expected level. The company"s ability to utilize assets for generation of sales had not been improved much during the study period as it was revealed by its turnover ratios.

1. **AUTHOR NAME** -: Praveen Kumar Jain
2. **YEAR-** : 1993
3. **REVIEW -:**

Conducted a study among seven paper companies in India to "Analyze the basic components of Working Capital" The study revealed that the current ratio in public sector undertakings during the study period was found to be highly erratic while the same in private sector undertakings registered continuous decrease. As far as the inventory was concerned, the study revealed that it was highly unplanned in public sector undertaking units when compared to private sector units. The study contributed much in terms of realizing the importance of effective management of working capital.

1. **AUTHOR NAME -**: Khan and Mohol Tutail Khan
2. **YEAR- :** 1990
3. **REVIEW -:**

In their study, "Paper Industry: An appraisal" pointed out that the paper industry is a highly capital intensive industry. Due to steady rise in the cost of inputs, heavy overheads, paucity of power and adverse impact of control orders over the industry, this industry has been unable to function vigorously. They have selected some of the important companies for the analysis during the period 1980-81 to 1985-86. The statistical analysis shows that the profitability of these companies during the period under review is not satisfactory. The profitability of these companies has been hampered because of controls over prices and production of printing paper. The study concluded that the control over price and production of printing paper should be removed.

1. **AUTHOR NAME -**: Kulkarni
2. **YEAR- :** 1989
3. **REVIEW -:**

In his article entitled "Paper and Paper Board" has examined the capacity utilization of the Indian Paper Industry during the two decades. He has observed that the capacity utilization declined very sharply from 823 per cent to 66.4 per cent during the first decade and to 60.41 per cent during the second decade of the study. He has further found the installed capacity was increased to 28.51 lakh tonnes per annum during the year 1988 as against the installed capacity of 9.54 lakh tonnes in the year 1971. The production of paper and paper boards was also increased in a similar manner as from 7.75 lakh tonnes to 17.20 lakh tones during the same period. Thus, it is noted that the capacity utilization of the paper industry has an inverse relationship with the installed capacity and production.

1. **AUTHOR NAME -**: Arun Ghosh
2. **YEAR- :** 1987
3. **REVIEW -:**

In his article entitled "Education and Environment Contribution of the Paper Industry" has reported that the growth of the paper industry was impressive and that the annual growth rate over the period 1951-1986 was 8.7 per cent for capacity and that of production, 7.4 per cent. He has observed that the overall capacity utilization had been declined from ninety six per cent in 1951 to sixty per cent in 1986. He has also observed that the capacity utilization was not in accordance with the growth of capacity of the paper industry.

1. AUTHOR NAME -: Bansal and Gupta
2. YEAR- : 1985
3. REVIEW -:

In their study entitled, "Financial Ratio Analysis and Statistics" enlightened that the coefficient of variation in the study period had a wide gap varying between 7.1 per cent and 51.3 per cent for current ratio and ratio of fixed assets to sales. The correlation of components of short term liquidity ratio generally possesses low correlation as against long term solvency ratio components but the components of both ratios independently possess quite satisfactory correlation in cotton textile industry. The profitability ratio elements in the industry also have quite high correlation in cotton industry as compared to synthetic industry

3.7 TITLE OF THE STUDY

After the review of literature and discussion with guide the researcher has finalized the following title of the study;

"FINANCIAL PARFORMANCE ANALYSIS OF TRADING HOUSES ON INDIA"

3.8 OBJECTIVES OF THE STDY

1   To know about trading houses in India.

2   To understand the ratio analysis

3   To analyzed liquidity ratio of selected samples during the study period

4   To analyzed working capital ratio of selected samples during the study period

5   To analyzed the asset ratio of selected sample during the study period

6   To analyzed the profitability ratio during the study period of selected samples.

7   To test the hypothesis to get conclusion of the study.

8. To provide valuable suggestion for the further scope and better improvement in this area of the study

3.9 HYPOTHESES OF THE STUDY

❖ **Null hypotheses**

1) There is no significant difference in current ratio of the sampled companies working as trading houses in India.

2) There is no significant difference in quick ratio of the sampled companies working as trading houses in India.

3) There is no significant in cash ratio of the sampled companies working as trading houses in India.

4) There is no significant deference in interval measure of the sampled companies working as trading houses in India.

5) There is no significant difference in Networking caption ration of the sampled companies working as trading houses in India.

6) There is no significant in inventor turn over ration of the sample companies working as trading houses in India.

7) There is no significant difference in inventory to working capital ratio of the sampled company working as trading houses in India.

8) There is no significant difference in debtor"s turnover of the sampled companies working as trading houses in India.

9) There is no significant difference in average collection period of the sampled companies working as trading houses in India.

10) There is no significant difference in current assets turnover ratio of the sampled companies working as trading houses in India.

❖ ALTERNATE HYPOTHESIS

1) There is significant difference in current ratio of the sampled companies working as trading houses in India.

2) There is significant difference in quick ratio of the sampled companies working as trading houses in India.

3) There is significant in cash ratio of the sampled companies working as trading houses in India.

4) There is significant deference in interval measure of the sampled companies working as trading houses in India.

5) There is significant difference in Networking caption ration of the sampled companies working as trading houses in India.

6) There is significant in inventory turnover ration of the sample companies working as trading houses in India.

7) There is significant difference in inventory to working capital ratio of the sampled company working as trading houses in India.

8) There is significant difference in debtor"s turnover of the sampled companies working as trading houses in India.

9) There is significant difference in average collection period of the sampled companies working as trading houses in India.

10) There is significant difference in current assets turnover ratio of the sampled companies working as trading houses in India.

There is significant in operating expense ratio of the sampled companies working as trading houses in India

3.10 UNIVERSE OF THE STUDY

All the trading houses are engaged in merchant activities in India are to be a part of Universe of the study.

3.11 SAMPLE OF THE STUDY

For this study researcher has selected 30 trading houses which are working in India for the merchandise business and involved in the trading activities in India.

3.12 SAMPLE TECHNIQUES

Researcher has selected convenient random sampling technique for the selection of the samples.

3.13 PERIOD OF THE STUDY

The present study is limited up to a period for 5 year from 2010 – 11 to 2015 – 16

3.14 SOURCES OF THE DATA

The study is based on secondary data related to the data was obtain from annual reports of a companies, magazines, journals, various bulletins and websites [moneycontrol.com, rediff.com, financialtime.com etc.]

3.15 DATA ANALYSIS

Taking in to consideration the cost, time and effort etc the data collected by the researcher.

The data has been collected from secondary sources about the liquidity, profitability, inventory and about ratios from various sources.

The data analysis will done with ANOVA.

3.16 TOOLS AND TECHNIQUES

For the purpose of data analysis following accounting tools and techniques as well as statistical tools and techniques has been applied like :

1. Ratio analysis

2. Average

3. F- test (ANOVA)

3.17 LIMITATION OF THE STUDY

This study concern following limitations

1. Only secondary data has been used for the study

2. Only limited time of 5 year which is period of the study has been taken for the analysis

3. Only 30 selected samples has been taken for conducting the study
4. Only one accounting tool which is ratio has been used for the data analysis.
5. There are two statistical tools are used only for the test of hypothesis (mean and F-TEST ANOVA)

3.18 SIGNIFICANCE OF THE STUDY

The study focuses mainly on the trading houses of India towards financial performance. It aims to analyze financial performance of trading houses and to do analysis of selected trading company.

1. Through this study knowledge of the researcher has improved
2. Investors get the idea about the trading houses.
3. This study will help to all the stakeholders for trading activity
4. This study creates further larger scop for the research in this particular area of the research.
5. This study will provide valuable suggestions to the trading house of the India for the better improvement in the merchant activity.

3.19 OUTLINE OF THE THESIS

3.19.1 Chapter 1 – Overview of trading houses and Sample profile

This chapter include - introduction, meaning of trading houses – definition of trading houses - classification of trading houses - criterion for recognition of trading houses - functions of trading houses - objectives of trading houses - assistance/incentives offered to trading houses by government of india - significance of trading houses - role of trading houses conclusion

3.19.2 Chapter 2 – Overview of financial performance

This Chapter is include Introduction and Concept of financial performance – meaning and definition of financial performance – financial analysis – operating ratio analysis – dupont analysis and measuring managerial performance – the importance of ratio analysis – factor affecting the efficiency of the ratios – analysis of financial statement – ratio analysis current ratio, quick ratio , operating ratio, etc – conclusion

3.19.3 Chapter 3 - Research Methodology

The Chapter is include Objectives of the Study and Hypothesis of the Study, this Chapter will also include the Methodology adopted for the Research - It will include the Universe of the Study - Sampling Design - Sampling Unit - Classification of Sampling - Data Collection & Analysis tools adopted for the study etc - This chapter will include Limitation, Important and Sources of Information used for the purpose of the Study.

3.19.4 Chapter 4 - Data Analysis & Interpretation

The various statistical tools are adopted for the data analysis and findings will be represented in form of charts and graphs. F - test ANOVAs and ratio analysis.

3.19.5 Chapter 5 - Summary Findings & Suggestions

This Chapter highlights General Criteria, Summary of Findings and Suggestions of the study and also suggested path for the Improvement and Future Areas for Research.

3.20 SCOP OF THE STUDY

All efforts have been made to ensure that the research is design and conducted to optimize the ability to achieve the research objective. However there are some constrains that do not validate the research but made to be acknowledge so there is still scope for the further study in this particular area as follow:-

- In this research the researcher have used 30 selected trading companies for analysis of financial performance of their financial statement and its interpretation
- Data collected for limited period of time which five year of data 2010-11 to 2015-16.
- Limited ratios are selected for the data analysis further so many information can be analyze through various techniques.
- Data collected is limited up to Indian companies only so this research can be reach to the national level which is major scope for analysis.

- The present study is largely based on Ratio Analysis and it has own limitations which also applies to the study.
- The researcher has also modified some of the formula used for the study, so its conclusion depends upon formulated ratio.
- The study should be based on thirty companies be long to private sector only and are listed on Bombay Stock Exchange.

❖ REFERENCES

➤ BOOKS

1. **C.R. Kothari**, "Research Methodology Methods & Techniques", Second Edition, New Delhi: New Age International Publisher, 2004, PP. 1-2.

2. **Malhotra Naresh k.** Marketing researches an applied orientation new Delhi, Dorling Kindersley India Pvt. ltd. License of person education in south Asia, 2006

3. **Sumit S.,** MBA 1st Year, Asm"s Institute of Business Management & Research, 2013

4. **B.E. Noltingk**, "The Human Element in Research Management", Third Printing, Amsterdam: Elsevier Publishing Company, 1965

➤ JOURNALS

1. Nizam Mohammed *"Indian Paper Industry: Heading for a Bright Future"* **1985**
2. Ramanchandran and Janakiraman „*working capital management efficiency and earnings before interest and tax of the paper industries in India.*" 2009
3. Burange & et al. *"Performance of Indian Cement Industry - The Competitive Landscape".* 2008

4 Adolphus *significant relationship between measure of liquidity and selected measures of profitability, efficiency and indebtedness in Nigerian quoted manufacturing companies.* 2008
5 Vijayasaradhi, S.P. *Problems of Working Capital Management in Public Enterprises,* Lok Udyog, January, 1981.
6 Vijayasaradhi, S.P, *Working Capital Management: A Conceptual Overview,* The Management Accountant, June 1981, p.273.
7 Wahi. A., *Organisation of Materials Management Function, Lok Udyog,* August 1980.
8 Walker, E. W., *Essentials of Financial Management,* New Delhi: Prentice Hall of India Pvt. Ltd., 1974.
9 Walker, E. W. *Essentials of Financial Management,* New Delhi: Prentice Hall of India, 1983.
10 Willets, W. E, *Fundamentals of Purchasing, New York*: Appleton Century Crafts, 1969.
11 Within, T. M, *Theory of Investment Management,* New Jersey: Princeton University Press, 1953.
12 Yadav, R. V, *Working Capital Management - A Parametric Approach,* The Chartered Accountant, Vol.23, No. 11, May 1986 pp. 952-955.
13 Zenoff, D. B. and Zack Zwick, *International Financial Management,* New Jersey: Prentice-Hall Inc., 1969Pandey, I. M., Financial Management, New Delhi, Vikas Publishing House Pvt. Ltd
14 Kathuria, S. (1996). Export Incentives: The Impact of Recent Policy Changes in India, *Indian Economic Review*, Vol. 31, No. 1, pp. 109-26.
15 Kaundal, R.K. (2005). *Trade Policy Reforms and Indian Exports*, Mahamaya Publishing House, New Delhi.
16 Kaundal, R.K (2006). Impact of Economic Reforms on External Sector, *Foreign Trade Review*, Vol. 38, No. 3, April-Sept., pp-72-99.
17 Kelkar, V K (2001). India"s Reform Agenda: Micro, Meso and Macro Economic Reforms, Fourth Annual Fellow Lecture, Centre for the Advanced Study of India, University of Pennsylvania
18 Khan, A. (2005). Barriers to Trade Under the WTO : A Special Case of Import Licensing and Rules of Origin, in Mittal J.K. and K.D. Raju (eds.), *World Trade*

Organization and India: A Critical Study of Its first Decade, New Era Law Publications, Delhi.

19 Kumar Rajiv & Gupta, Abhijit Sen (2008), Towards A Competitive Manufacturing Sector, ICRIER Working Paper No. 203

20 Kumar, Pranav (2005). "Services Negotiations in the Doha Round: Concerns of South Asia", *World Development Indicators*, Presented on 9-10 March, World Bank, Colombo.

21 Kumar, R. and Sengupta,A. (2008). Towards A Competitive Manufacturing Sector. ICRIER Working Paper No. 203.

22 Lakshmanan, L., Chinngaihlian, S. and Rajesh R. (2007). Competitiveness of India"s Manufacturing Sector: An Assessment of Related Issues. Reserve Bank of India *Occasional Papers*, Vol. 28, No. 1.

23 Marjit, Sugata and Chaudary Roy, A.(1997). *India's Exports*, Oxford University Press, New Delhi.

24 Meier, G.M. "Trade policy Development", in Scott Maurice and lal Deepak (ed.), *Public Policy and Economic Development,* (Oxford, 1990), p.159

25 Anderson, James E. and Douglas Marcouiller. Forthcoming. *"Insecurity, and the Pattern of Trade: An Empirical Investigation,"* Rev. Econ. Statist.

26 Belderbos, René and Leo Sleuwaegen. 1998. *"Tariff Jumping DFI and Export Substitution: Japanese Electronics Firms in Europe,"* Int. J. Ind. Org. 16, pp. 601–38.

27 Bergstrand, Jeffrey H. 1985. *"The Gravity Equation in International Trade: Some Microeconomic Foundations and Empirical Evidence,"* Rev. Econ. Stat. 67, pp. 474–81.

28 Bernard, Andrew B. and Bradford J. Jensen. 1999. *"Exceptional Exporter Performance: Cause, Effect, or Both?"* J. Int. Econ. 47:1, pp. 1–25.

CHAPTER 4
DATA ANALYSIS AND INTERPRETATION

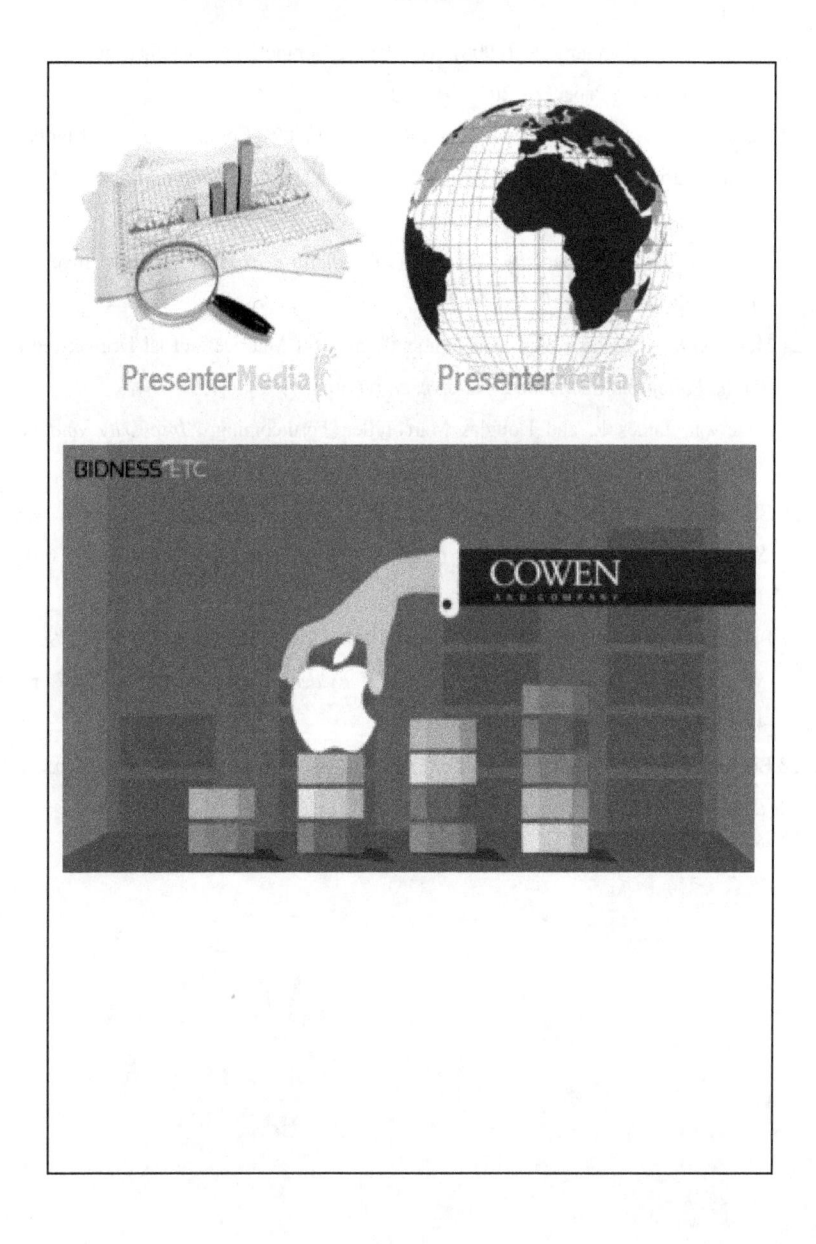

INDEX

SR NO.	CONTAIN	PAGE NO.
4.1	INTRODUCTION	108
4.2	STANDARD OF COMPARISON	108
❖	CURRENT RATIO	108
❖	QUICK RATIO	112
❖	CASH RATIO	115
❖	INTERVAL MEASURE	119
❖	NETWORKING CAPITAL RATIO	121
❖	INVENTORY TURNOVER	124
❖	INVENTORY WORKING CAPITAL RATIO	128
❖	DEBTORS TURNOVER	131
❖	AVERAGE COLLECTION PERIOD	134
❖	CURRENT ASSETS TURNOVER	137
❖	WORKING CAPITAL TURNOVER RATIO	140
❖	GROSS PROFITABILITY RATIO	143
❖	NET PROFITABILITY RATIO	147
4.3	CONCLUSION	150

SR.NO.	LIST OF TABLE	PAGE NO
4.1	Current Ratio of Sampled Trading Houses	108
4.2	Abstract of F-Test	111
4.3	Result of F-Test	112
4.4	Quick Ratio of Sampled Trading Houses	114
4.5	Abstract of F-Test	115
4.6	Result of F-Test	116
4.7	Cash Ratio of Sampled Trading Houses	117
4.8	Abstract of F-Test	118
4.9	Result of F-Test	119
4.10	Interval Measure of Sampled Trading Houses	120
4.11	Abstract of F-Test	121
4.12	Result of F-Test	122
4.13	Net Working Capital Ratio of Sampled Trading Houses	123
4.14	Abstract of F-Test	124
4.15	Result of F-Test	126
4.16	Inventory Turnover Ratio of Sampled Trading Houses 188	127
4.17	Abstract of F-Test	129
4.18	Result of F-Test	130
4.19	Inventory to Working Capital Ratio of Sampled Trading Houses	131
4.20	Abstract of F-Test	132
4.21	Result of F-Test	133
4.22	Debtors Turnover Ratio of Sampled Trading Houses	136
4.23	Abstract of F-Test	137
4.24	Result of F-Test	138
4.25	Average Collection Period of Sampled Trading Houses	140
4.26	Abstract of F-Test	141
4.27	Result of F-Test	142
4.28	Current Assets Turnover Ratio of Sampled Trading Houses	143
4.29	Abstract of F-Test	144
4.30	Result of F-Test	145

4.31	Working Capital Turnover Ratio of Sampled Trading Houses	**146**
4.32	Abstract of F-Test	**147**
4.33	Result of F-Test	**148**
4.34	Gross Profit Margin of Sampled Trading Houses	**149**
4.35	Abstract of F-Test	**150**
4.36	Result of F-Test	**151**
4.37	Net Profit Margin of Sampled Trading Houses	**152**
4.38	Abstract of F-Test	**153**
4.39	Result of F-Test	**154**
4.40	Operating Expense Ratio of Sampled Trading Houses	**155**
4.41	Abstract of F-Test	**156**
4.42	Result of F-Test	**157**

4.1 INTRODUCTION

The researcher has examined working capital ratios for the purpose of analysis of working management of sampled companies under study. Ratio analysis is powerful tool of financial analysis. A ratio is defined as "the indicated quotient of two mathematical expressions." and as "the relationship between two or more things." In financial analysis, a ratio is used as a benchmark for evaluating the financial position and performance of a firm. The relationship between two accounting figures, expressed mathematically, is known as a financial ratio or simply as ratio. Ratio helps to summarize the large qualitative judgement about the firm's financial performance.

4.2 STANDARDS OF COMPARISON:

The ratio analysis involves comparison for a useful interpretation of the financial statement. A single ratio in itself does not indicate favourable or unfavourable condition. It should be compared with some standard. Standards of comparison may consist of:

- ❖ **Past ratios**, i.e. ratios calculated from the past financial statements of the same firm;
- ❖ **Projected ratios**, i.e. ratios developed using the projected, or proforma, financial statement of the same firm;
- ❖ **Competitor's ratios**, i.e. ratios of some selected firms, especially the most progressive and successful competitor, at the same point in time, and
- ❖ **Industry ratios**, i.e. ratio of the industry of which the firm belongs.

❖ **CURRENT RATIO:**

The current ratio is calculated by dividing current assets by current liabilities :

$$\text{Current Ratio} = \frac{\text{Current Assets}}{\text{Current Liabilities}}$$

Current assets include cash and those assets which can be converted in to cash within years, such as marketable securities, debtors and inventories. Prepaid expenses are also included in current assets as they represent the payments that will not be made by the firm in the future. All obligations maturing within a year include in current liabilities.

Current liabilities include creditors, bills payable, accrued expenses, short-term bank loan, income-tax liability and long-term debt maturing in current year. The current ratio is measure of form's short-term solvency. The availability of current assets in rupees for every one rupee of current liability, A ratio of greater than one means that the firm has more current assets than current claims against them.

The researcher has taken the following item in current ratio of sampled companies working as trading houses in India.

- ❖ Current assets =Inventories, Sundry Debtors, Cash & Bank Balance. and short-term loan & Advances.
- ❖ Current liabilities = Current liabilities and provisions.

The researcher has examined current ratio of 30 Trading houses for the period of 2011-2012 to 2015-16. The summary of current ratio of selected trading houses is as follows:

The following table 4.1 indicates current ratio of sampled companies working as Trading Houses in India for the period of 2011-2012 to 2015-16.

Table – 4.1
Current Ratio of Sampled Trading Houses

SR. NO	Trading Houses	2011–2012	2012-2013	2013-2014	2014-2015	2015-2016	Average
1	Adani Enterprise	6.03	5.68	2.72	2.91	2.98	**4.06**
2	MMTC ltd	1.86	1.52	1.38	1.31	1.89	**1.59**
3	PTC India	1.63	1.44	1.74	1.43	1.60	**1.57**
4	Swan energy	1.56	3.35	1.64	2.43	2.22	**2.24**
5	Andrew Yule	12.67	10.48	18.04	12.40	13.02	**13.32**
6	STC India	8.32	4.32	6.81	8.06	6.38	**6.78**
7	Shaily India	2.22	3.02	2.51	2.39	2.36	**2.50**
8	Ind motor parts	2.39	3.67	2.00	2.42	1.88	**2.47**
9	Uniphos Ent	10.56	9.76	6.49	6.24	6.50	**7.91**
10	Grandeur Prod	11.59	8.66	17.38	9.09	7.20	**10.78**
11	Control print	1.92	2.27	1.97	1.98	2.01	**2.03**
12	Apollo Tricoat	1.82	5.70	2.93	2.74	5.67	**3.77**
13	Sat Ind	1.77	2.85	2.59	2.77	1.81	**2.36**
14	Singer India	2.12	2.41	1.86	2.33	1.90	**2.12**
15	Urja Global	1.14	0.81	0.97	1.18	0.88	**1.00**
16	Competent Auto	1.09	1.03	1.30	1.42	1.12	**1.19**
17	High Ground Ent	1.28	0.89	1.28	1.27	0.99	**1.14**
18	Cravatex	0.61	0.72	0.77	0.72	0.71	**0.71**
19	Lahoti Over	2.29	2.13	2.57	2.85	2.19	**2.41**
20	Tandl Global	1.82	4.61	1.82	1.67	2.88	**2.56**
21	Bombay cycle	3.27	2.24	2.98	2.47	1.53	**2.50**
22	Mishka Exim	2.15	2.26	2.18	2.03	1.91	**2.11**
23	ABans enetrpris	2.55	8.83	2.25	3.09	2.98	**3.94**
24	Starlite compo	2.79	3.26	3.42	3.48	2.96	**3.18**
25	CCL int.	3.17	2.94	2.30	2.67	2.52	**2.72**
26	WH brady	2.75	3.45	2.39	2.28	3.14	**2.80**
27	Maximaa Systems	0.88	0.52	1.04	1.15	0.82	**0.88**
28	Mystic Electr	2.87	3.36	2.65	2.28	3.47	**2.93**
29	Gayatri bio	1.35	1.62	1.38	1.20	1.34	**1.38**
30	Empower India	1.64	0.86	1.73	1.93	1.53	**1.54**
	Average	3.27	3.49	3.37	3.01	2.95	

(SOURCE – WWW.MONEYCONTROL.COM AND EXCEL)

F-Test (ANOVA) Analysis:

The researcher has applied the two-way analysis of variance (F-Test) to judge the significance variance in company - wise and year-wise current ratio of sampled companies working as Trading Houses in India. Abstract of F-Test is shown in table 4.2. The summary of the results of the analysis of variance test is shown in table - 4.3.

	Table no 4.3 Abstract of F-Test				
SR. NO	SUMMARY	Count	Sum	Average	Variance
1	Adani eneterpris	5	20.32	4.064	2.89743
2	MMTC ltd	5	7.98	1.592	0.07257
3	PTC India	5	7.84	1.568	0.01747
4	Swan energy	5	11.2	2.24	0.52275
5	Andrew yule	5	66.61	13.322	7.92572
6	STC India	5	33.89	6.778	2.55582
7	Shaily India	5	12.5	2.5	0.09515
8	Ind motor parts	5	12.36	2.472	0.50447
9	Uniphos Ent	5	39.55	7.91	4.3096
10	Grandeur Prod	5	53.92	10.784	16.09573
11	Control print	5	10.15	2.03	0.01905
12	Apollo Tricoat	5	18.88	3.772	3.22597
13	Sat Ind	5	11.79	2.358	0.27792
14	Singer India	5	10.62	2.124	0.06103
15	Urja Global	5	4.98	0.996	0.02583
16	Competent Auto	5	5.98	1.192	0.02637
17	High Ground Ent	5	5.71	1.142	0.03527
18	Cravatex	5	3.53	0.706	0.00343
19	Lahoti Over	5	12.03	2.406	0.09008
20	Tandl Global	5	12.8	2.56	1.54805
21	Bombay cycle	5	12.49	2.498	0.45817
22	Mishka Exim	5	10.53	2.106	0.01883
23	ABans enetrpris	5	19.7	3.94	7.5861
24	Starlite compo	5	15,91	3.182	0.08862
25	CCL int.	5	13.6	2.72	0.11745
26	WH brady	5	14.01	2.802	0.24477
27	Maximaa Systems	5	4.41	0.882	0.05792
28	Mystic Electr	5	14.63	2.926	0.24523
29	Gayatri bio	5	6.95	1.39	0.0311
30	Empower India	5	7.69	1.538	0.16517
	Year-2011-2012	30	90.19	3.006333	6.749148
	Year-2012-2013	30	101.09	3.369687	16.98244
	Year-2013-2014	30	98.11	3.270333	10.30033
	Year-2014-2015	30	88.39	2.946333	6.527679
	Year-2015-2016	30	104.72	3.490667	7.532482

(SOURCE – WWW.MONEYCONTROL.COM AND EXCEL)

Table - 4.3

Result of F-Test

Source of Variation	SS	DF	MSS	F-Cal. Value	5% F Limit
Companies	1204.739	29	41.54273	25.37215	1.565322
Years	6.56056	4	1.64014	1.001713	2.44988
Error	189.9309	116	1.637336		
Total	1401.231	149			

(SOURCE – WWW.MONEYCONTROL.COM AND EXCEL)

From the Table - 4.3 it is observed that:

Calculated F-Value is statistically greater than the F-Table Value at 5% significance level. Therefore the result of the F-Test rejects the null hypothesis.

H_1 So we conclude that there is significant variation among company-wise current assets ratio of sampled companies working as Trading Houses in India.

H_0 So we conclude that there is no significant variation among year-wise current ratio of sampled companies working as Trading Houses in India.

❖ QUICK RATIO :

This ratio establishes a relationship between quick or liquid assets and current liabilities. An assets is liquid, if it can be converted into cash immediately or reasonably soon without a loss of value. Cash is the most liquid asset. Other assets which are considered to be relatively liquid and included in quick assets are book debts (debtors and bills receivables) and marketable securities (temporary quoted investments.)Inventories are considered to be less liquid. Inventories normally require some time for realising into cash; their value also has a tendency to fluctuate. The quick ratio of sampled Trading Houses is found out by dividing quick assets by current liabilities.

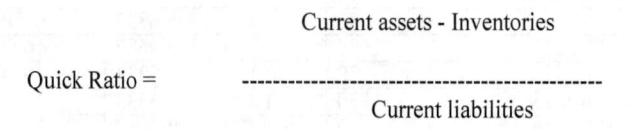

$$\text{Quick Ratio} = \frac{\text{Current assets - Inventories}}{\text{Current liabilities}}$$

Generally a quick ratio of 1:1 is considered to represent a satisfactory current financial condition.

The researcher has examined quick ratio of 30 Trading houses for the period of 2011-2012 to 2015-16. The summary of quick ratio of selected Trading Houses is as follows:

The following table 6.4 indicates quick ratio of sampled companies working as Trading Houses in India for the period of 2011-2012 to 2015-16.

Table - 4.4

Quick Ratio of Sampled Trading Houses

SR. NO	Trading Houses	2011-12	2012-13	2013-14	2014-15	2015-16	Average
1	Adani eneterpris	1.56	1.18	1.98	1.53	1.39	1.53
2	MMTC ltd	1.00	1.01	1.27	1.39	0.97	1.13
3	PTC India	1.01	1.20	1.25	1.17	0.95	1.12
4	Swan energy	1.12	0.65	0.78	1.28	1.98	1.16
5	Andrew yule	8.54	12.63	9.04	8.26	7.25	9.14
6	STC India	3.77	2.95	4.27	2.91	2.11	3.20
7	Shaily India	1.09	1.35	1.37	1.44	2.05	1.46
8	Ind motor parts	1.51	1.14	1.62	1.23	2.33	1.57
9	Uniphos Ent	1.60	2.11	3.17	1.74	3.69	2.46
10	Grandeur Prod	1.84	4.20	3.19	1.86	2.81	2.78
11	Control print	1.17	1.07	1.16	1.15	1.32	1.17
12	Apollo Tricoat	1.64	1.99	1.21	5.07	5.04	2.99
13	Sat Ind	2.25	2.16	1.18	1.14	2.19	1.78
14	Singer India	1.33	0.74	1.00	0.88	1.29	1.05
15	Urja Global	0.96	0.73	0.92	0.66	0.67	0.79
16	Competent Auto	0.96	0.88	0.67	0.57	0.57	0.73
17	High Ground Ent	1.06	0.95	1.04	0.61	0.59	0.85
18	Cravatex	0.49	0.57	0.40	0.43	0.40	0.46
19	Lahoti Over	1.48	1.31	1.06	1.29	1.22	1.27
20	Tandl Global	1.12	0.97	0.99	1.45	2.91	1.49
21	Bombay cycle	2.25	2.55	2.57	0.96	1.28	1.92
22	Mishka Exim	1.53	1.20	1.26	1.18	1.45	1.32
23	ABans enetrpris	1.59	1.38	1.69	2.18	7.94	2.96
24	Starlite compo	1.72	1.59	1.21	1.24	1.49	1.45
25	CCL int.	1.48	1.03	1.37	1.22	1.78	1.38
26	WH brady	1.41	1.54	1.87	2.18	2.26	1.85
27	Maximaa Systems	0.71	0.52	0.35	0.37	0.35	0.46
28	Mystic Electr	1.20	1.15	1.52	1.97	2.14	1.60
29	Gayatri bio	0.89	0.93	0.91	0.85	1.06	0.93
30	Empower India	1.63	1.40	1.36	1.27	0.58	1.25
	Average	1.66	1.77	1.72	1.65	2.07	

(SOURCE – WWW.MONEYCONTROL.COM AND EXCEL)

F-Test (ANOVA) Analysis:

The researcher has applied the two-way analysis of variance (F-Test) to judge the significance variance in company - wise and year-wise quick ratio of sampled companies working as Trading Houses in India. Abstract of F-Test is shown in table 4.5. The summary of the results of the analysis of variance test is shown in table - 4.6.

Table - 4.5 Abstract of F-Test

SR. NO.	SUMMARY	Count	Sum	Average	Variance
1	Adani eneterpris	5	7.84	1.528	0.08637
2	MMTC ltd	5	5.64	1.128	0.03602
3	PTC India	5	5.58	1.116	0.01668
4	Swan energy	5	5.81	1.162	0.27322
5	Andrew yule	5	45.72	9.144	4.22413
6	STC India	5	16.01	3.202	0.70112
7	Shaily India	5	7.3	1.46	0.1264
8	Ind motor parts	5	7.83	1.566	0.22103
9	Uniphos Ent	5	12.31	2.482	0.84937
10	Grandeur Prod	5	13.9	2.78	0.97885
11	Control print	5	5.87	1.174	0.00823
12	Apollo Tricoat	5	14.95	2.99	3.62995
13	Sat Ind	5	8.92	1.784	0.32573
14	Singer India	5	5.24	1.048	0.06587
15	Urja Global	5	3.94	0.788	0.02017
16	Competent Auto	5	3.65	0.73	0.03255
17	High Ground Ent	5	4.25	0.85	0.05385
18	Cravatex	5	2.29	0.458	0.00527
19	Lahoti Over	5	8.36	1.272	0.02317
20	Tandl Global	5	7.44	1.488	0.66882
21	Bombay cycle	5	9.61	1.922	0.56487
22	Mishka Exim	5	6.62	1.324	0.02463
23	ABans enetrpris	5	14.78	2.956	7.84873
24	Starlite compo	5	7.25	1.45	0.04895
25	CCL int.	5	6.88	1.376	0.07953
26	WH brady	5	9.26	1.852	0.14177
27	Maximaa Systems	5	2.3	0.46	0.0246
28	Mystic Electr	5	7.98	1.596	0.19933
29	Gayatri bio	5	4.64	0.928	0.00832
30	Empower India	5	6.24	1.248	0.15707
	Year-2011-2012	30	49.91	1.6636667	2.0426171
	Year-2012-2013	30	53.08	1.7693333	4.8112961
	Year-2013-2014	30	51.68	1.7226867	2.8274961
	Year-2014-2015	30	49.48	1.6493333	2.3387851
	Year-2015-2016	30	62.06	2.0686667	3.3019982

(SOURCE – WWW.MONEYCONTROL.COM AND EXCEL)

Table - 4.6

Result of F-Test

Source of Variation	SS	DF	MSS	F-Cal. Value	5% F Limit
Companies	356.2885	29	12.285812	17.326162	1.56532169
Years	3.515936	4	0.878984	1.239594	2.44988031
Error	82.25448	116	0.7090902		
Total	442.0589	149			

(SOURCE – WWW.MONEYCONTROL.COM AND EXCEL)

From the Table - 4.6 it is observed that:

H_1 Calculated F-Value is statistically greater than the F-Table Value at 5% significance level. Therefore the result of the F-Test rejects the null hypothesis. So we conclude that there is significant variation among company- wise quick ratio of sampled companies working as Trading Houses in India.

H_0 F-Calculated value is statistically less than F-Table value at 5% significance level. Therefore the result of the F-Test accepts the null hypothesis. So we conclude that there is no significant variation among year-wise quick ratio of sampled companies working as Trading Houses in India.

❖ **CASH RATIO:**

This ratio establishes a relationship between cash and current Liabilities of sampled companies working as Trading Houses in India.. Cash is the most liquid asset. Trade investment or marketable securities are equivalent of cash; therefore, they may be included in the computation of cash ratio of sampled Trading Houses. Cash ratio is calculated as per follows:

$$\text{Cash Ratio} = \frac{\text{Cash + Marketable securities}}{\text{Current liabilities}}$$

The researcher has examined cash ratio of 30 Trading houses for the period of 2011-2012 to 2015-16. The summaries of cash ratio of selected Trading Houses are as follows:

The following table 4.7 indicates cash ratio of sampled companies working as Trading Houses in India for the period of 2011-2012 to 2015-16.

Table - 4.7
Cash Ratio of Sampled Trading Houses

SR. NO	Trading Houses	2011-12	2012-13	2013-14	2014-15	2015-16	Average
1	Adani eEnterprise	0.113	0.079	0.253	0.758	0.085	0.2576
2	MMTC ltd	0.11	0.124	0.575	0.535	0.37	0.3428
3	PTC India	0.025	0.048	0.014	0.029	0.053	0.0338
4	Swan energy	0.049	0.043	0.037	0.043	0.552	0.1448
5	Andrew yule	0.874	1.766	1.178	0.833	1.019	1.134
6	STC India	0.108	0.039	0.148	0.178	0.049	0.1044
7	Shaily India	0.026	0.012	0.032	0.014	0.635	0.1438
8	Ind motor parts	0.02	0.032	0.115	0.082	0.85	0.2198
9	Uniphos Ent	0.091	0.284	0.791	0.187	1.077	0.486
10	Grandeur Prod	0.13	0.224	0.205	0.075	0.6	0.2468
11	Control print	0.031	0.02	0.008	0.012	0.044	0.023
12	Apollo Tricoat	0.208	0.473	0.286	2.876	3.109	1.3904
13	Sat Ind	0.079	0.044	0.041	0.047	0.959	0.234
14	Singer India	0.266	0.093	0.087	0.052	0.028	0.1052
15	Urja Global	0.065	0.09	0.28	0.106	0.029	0.114
16	Competent Auto	0.027	0.019	0.03	0.154	0.021	0.0502
17	High Ground Ent	0.008	0.005	0.009	0.061	0.032	0.023
18	Cravatex	0.047	0.064	0.042	0.0361	0.041	0.04602
19	Lahoti Over	0.069	0.539	0.04	0.04	0.03	0.1436
20	Tandl Global	0.033	0.028	0.034	0.039	0.267	0.0802
21	Bombay cycle	0.069	0.101	0.546	0.35	0.395	0.2922
22	Mishka Exim	0.111	0.03	0.064	0.047	0.049	0.0602
23	ABans enetrpris	0.427	0.181	0.277	0.399	6.158	1.4884
24	Starlite compo	0.208	0.195	0.223	0.126	0.23	0.1964
25	CCL int.	0.115	0.074	0.081	0.055	0.551	0.1752
26	WII brady	0.03	0.065	0.081	0.063	0.096	0.067
27	Maximaa Systems	0.027	0.007	0.009	0.026	0.013	0.0164
28	Mystic Electr	0.022	0.014	0.015	0.084	0.042	0.0354
29	Gayatri bio	0.144	0.204	0.175	0.163	0.312	0.1996
30	Empower India	0.102	0.125	0.063	0.048	0.06	0.0796
	Average	0.121133	0.1674	0.1913	0.250603	0.591867	

(SOURCE – WWW.MONEYCONTROL.COM AND EXCEL)

F-Test (ANOVA) Analysis:

The researcher has applied the two-way analysis of variance (F-Test) to judge the significance variance in company - wise and year-wise cash ratio of sampled companies working as Trading Houses in India. Abstract of F-Test is shown in table 4.8 The summary of the results of the analysis of variance test is shown in table - 4.9

Table - 4.8
Abstract of F-Test

SR NO	SUMMARY	Count	Sum	Average	Variance
1	Adani eneterpris	5	1.288	0.2576	0.083255
2	MMTC ltd	5	1.714	0.3428	0.048417
3	PTC India	5	0.169	0.0338	0.000266
4	Swan energy	5	0.724	0.1448	0.051834
5	Andrew Yule	5	5.87	1.134	0.143197
6	STC India	5	0.522	0.1044	0.003669
7	Shaily India	5	0.719	0.1438	0.075488
8	Ind motor parts	5	1.099	0.2198	0.125578
9	Uniphos Ent	5	2.43	0.486	0.182134
10	Grandeur Prod	5	1.234	0.2468	0.042544
11	Control print	5	0.115	0.023	0.000215
12	Apollo Tricoat	5	6.952	1.3904	2.154996
13	Sat Ind	5	1.17	0.234	0.164492
14	Singer India	5	0.526	0.1052	0.008782
15	Urja Global	5	0.57	0.114	0.009456
16	Competent Auto	5	0.251	0.0502	0.003387
17	High Ground Ent	5	0.115	0.023	0.000568
18	Cravatex	5	0.2301	0.04602	0.000116
19	Lahoti Over	5	0.718	0.1436	0.049069
20	Tandl Global	5	0.401	0.0802	0.01092
21	Bombay cycle	5	1.461	0.2922	0.041175
22	Mishka Exim	5	0.301	0.0602	0.000952
23	ABans enetrpris	5	7.442	1.4884	6.823828
24	Starlite compo	5	0.982	0.1964	0.001732
25	CCL int.	5	0.876	0.1752	0.044803
26	WH brady	5	0.335	0.067	0.000607
27	Maximaa Systems	5	0.082	0.0164	8.98E-05
28	Mystic Electr	5	0.177	0.0354	0.000865
29	Gayatri bio	5	0.998	0.1996	0.004422
30	Empower India	5	0.398	0.0796	0.001055
	Year-2011-2012	30	3.834	0.121133	0.023033
	Year-2012-2013	30	5.022	0.1674	0.10776
	Year-2013-2014	30	5.739	0.1913	0.070399
	Year-2014-2015	30	7.5181	0.250603	0.290187

| | | Year-2015-2016 | | 30 | 17.756 | 0.591867 | 1.477287 |

(SOURCE – WWW.MONEYCONTROL.COM AND EXCEL)

Result of F-Test

Source of Variation	SS	DF	MSS	F-Cal. Value	5% F Limit
Companies	21.20681	29	0.731263	2.35435	1.565322
Years	4.281031	4	1.07027	3.445308	2.44988
Error	36.02968	116	0.310601		
Total	61.51737	149			

(SOURCE – WWW.MONEYCONTROL.COM AND EXCEL)

From the Table- 4.9 it is observed that:

H_0 — Calculated F-Value is statistically greater than the F-Table Value at 5% significance level. Therefore the result of the F-Test rejects the null hypothesis. So we conclude that there is significant variation among company-wise cash ratio of sampled companies working as Trading Houses in India.

H_1 — Calculated F-Value is statistically greater than the F-Table Value at 5% significance level. Therefore the result of the F-Test rejects the null hypothesis. So we conclude that there is significant variation among year-wise cash ratio of sampled companies working as Trading Houses in India.

❖ **INTERVAL MEASURE :**

Interval measure assesses sampled Trading Houses ability to Meet its regular cash expenses. It relates liquid assets to average daily operating cash out flows. The daily operating expenses will be equal to cost of goods sold plus selling, administrative and general expenses less depreciation (and other non-cash expenditures) divided by number of days in the year.

$$\text{Interval Measure} = \frac{\text{Current assets-Inventory}}{\text{Average daily operating expenses}}$$

The researcher has examined interval measure of 30 Trading houses for the period of 2011-2012 to 2015-16. The summaries of interval measure of selected Trading Houses are as follows:

The following table 4.10 indicates interval measure of sampled companies working as Trading Houses in India for the period of 2011-2012 to 2015-16.

Table - 4.10

Interval Measure of Sampled Trading Houses

SR NO.	Trading Houses	2011-12	2012-13	2013-14	2014-15	2015-16	Average
1	Adani eneterpris	43	36	35	48	21	36.6
2	MMTC ltd	66	61	107	102	75	82.2
3	PTC India	133	127	135	150	111	131.2
4	Swan energy	145	104	139	196	246	166
5	Andrew Yule	207	186	195	181	192	192.2
6	STC India	148	135	162	135	169	149.8
7	Shaily India	138	153	177	203	303	194.8
8	Ind motor parts	139	113	239	190	286	193.4
9	Uniphos Ent	44	54	64	76	125	72.6
10	Grandeur Prod	52	60	62	66	100	68
11	Control print	194	207	210	198	200	201.8
12	Apollo Tricoat	148	223	177	644	543	347
13	Sat Ind	322	339	154	149	269	246.6
14	Singer India	221	134	151	199	284	197.8
15	Urja Global	93	58	83	67	142	88.6
16	Competent Auto	125	128	94	78	77	100.4
17	High Ground Ent	158	118	156	99	139	134
18	Cravatex	148	180	117	123	109	135.4
19	Lahoti Over	129	131	116	123	137	127.2
20	Tandl Global	151	98	81	72	112	102.8
21	Bombay cycle	413	307	258	219	170	273.4
22	Mishka Exim	95	100	82	100	131	101.6
23	ABans enetrpris	186	269	327	355	1314	490.2
24	Starlite compo	110	79	78	76	94	87.4
25	CCL int.	155	127	119	116	203	144
26	WH brady	148	157	160	195	188	169.6
27	Maximaa Systems	144	109	76	63	61	90.6
28	Mystic Electr	82	68	72	81	96	79.8
29	Gayatri bio	127	111	112	98	114	112.4
30	Empower India	264	228	224	201	81	199.6
	Average	150.9333	140	138.7333	153.4333	203.0667	

(SOURCE – WWW.MONEYCONTROL.COM AND EXCEL)

F-Test (ANOVA) Analysis:

The researcher has applied the two-way analysis of variance (F-Test) to judge the significance variance in company - wise and year-wise interval measure of sampled companies working as Trading Houses in India. Abstract of F-Test is shown in table 4.11. The summary of the results of the analysis of variance test is shown in table - 4.12.

Table - 4.11

Abstract of F-Test

SR NO.	SUMMARY	Count	Sum	Average	Variance
1	Adani eneterpris	5	183	36.6	104.3
2	MMTC ltd	5	411	82.2	442.7
3	PTC India	5	656	131.2	199.2
4	Swan energy	5	830	166	3078.5
5	Andrew Yule	5	961	192.2	97.7
6	STC India	5	749	149.8	239.7
7	Shaily India	5	974	194.8	4266.2
8	Ind motor parts	5	967	193.4	5022.3
9	Uniphos Ent	5	363	72.6	998.8
10	Grandeur Prod	5	340	68	346
11	Control print	5	1009	201.8	43.2
12	Apollo Tricoat	5	1735	347	52625.5
13	Sat Ind	5	1233	246.6	8206.3
14	Singer India	5	989	197.8	3557.7
15	Urja Global	5	443	88.6	1076.3
16	Competent Auto	5	502	100.4	614.3
17	High Ground Ent	5	670	134	641.5
18	Cravatex	5	677	135.4	834.3
19	Lahoti Over	5	636	127.2	64.2
20	Tandl Global	5	514	102.8	963.7
21	Bombay cycle	5	1367	273.4	8626.3
22	Mishka Exim	5	508	101.6	324.3
23	ABans enetrpris	5	2451	490.2	216256.7
24	Starlite compo	5	437	87.4	210.8
25	CCL int.	5	720	144	1325
26	WH brady	5	848	169.6	425.3
27	Maximaa Systems	5	453	90.6	1260.3
28	Mystic Electr	5	399	79.8	117.2
29	Gayatri bio	5	562	112.4	106.3
30	Empower India	5	998	199.6	4904.3
	Year-2011-2012	30	4528	150.9333	6117.375
	Year-2012-2013	30	4200	140	5593.379
	Year-2013-2014	30	4162	138.7333	4445.72
	Year-2014-2015	30	4603	153.4333	13073.56
	Year-2015-2016	30	6092	203.0667	54258.27

(SOURCE – WWW.MONEYCONTROL.COM AND EXCEL)

Table - 4.12

Result of F-Test

Source of Variation	SS	DF	MSS	F-Cal. Value	5% F Limit
Companies	1237067	29	42657.49	4.17895	1.565322
Years	83821.87	4	20955.47	2.052907	2.44988
Error	1184094	116	10207.7		
Total	2504983	149			

(SOURCE – WWW.MONEYCONTROL.COM AND EXCEL)

From the Table- 4.12 it is observed that:

H_1 Calculated F-Value is statistically greater than the F-Table Value at 5% significance level. Therefore the result of the F-Test rejects the null hypothesis. So we conclude that there is significant variation among company-wise interval measure of sampled companies working as Trading Houses in India.

H_0 Calculated F-Value is statistically less than the F-Table Value at 5% significance level. Therefore the result of the F-Test accepts the null hypothesis. So we conclude that there is no significant variation among year-wise interval measure of sampled companies working as Trading Houses in India.

❖ NET WORKING CAPITAL RATIO:

The difference between current assets and current liabilities excluding short-term borrowing is called net working capital (NWC) or net current assets (NCA). Net working capital is used as a measure of Trading Houses liquidity. It is considered that, between two firms, the one having the larger NWC has the greater ability to meet its current obligations.

$$\text{NWC Ratio} = \frac{\text{Net working capital}}{\text{Net assets}}$$

The researcher has examined net working capital ratio of 30 Trading houses for the period of 2011-2012 to 2015-16. The summaries of net working capital ratio of selected trading houses are as follows:

The following table 4.13 indicates net working capital ratio of sampled companies working as Trading Houses in India for the period of 2011-2012 to 2015-16.

Table - 4.13

Net Working Capital Ratio of Sampled Trading Houses

SR. NO	Trading Houses	2011-12	2012-13	2013-14	2014-15	2015-16	Average
1	Adani eneterpris	0.03	0.337	0.635	0.496	0.523	0.4042
2	MMTC ltd	0.457	0.493	0.677	0.623	0.442	0.5384
3	PTC India	0.377	0.452	0.463	0.368	0.295	0.391
4	Swan energy	0.188	0.166	0.165	0.286	0.43	0.247
5	Andrew yule	0.974	0.975	0.956	0.944	0.934	0.9566
6	STC India	0.856	0.836	0.862	0.845	0.851	0.85
7	Shaily India	0.282	0.343	0.325	0.34	0.465	0.351
8	Ind motor parts	0.325	0.278	0.331	0.189	0.381	0.3008
9	Uniphos Ent	0.787	0.769	0.746	0.764	0.755	0.7642
10	Grandeur Prod	0.877	0.876	0.856	0.845	0.836	0.858
11	Control print	0.52	0.548	0.395	0.505	0.524	0.4984
12	Apollo Tricoat	0.387	0.455	0.187	0.495	0.58	0.4208
13	Sat Ind	0.511	0.511	0.341	0.321	0.564	0.4496
14	Singer India	0.279	0.202	0.234	0.238	0.306	0.2518
15	Urja Global	0.022	-0.003	0.019	-0.017	-0.035	-0.0028
16	Competent Auto	0.086	0.07	0.02	0.03	0.008	0.0428
17	High Ground Ent	0.049	0.075	0.12	-0.002	-0.038	0.0408
18	Cravatex	-0.18	-0.179	-0.298	-0.236	-0.159	-0.2104
19	Lahoti Over	0.486	0.43	0.402	0.307	0.275	0.38
20	Tandl Global	0.319	0.263	0.221	0.378	0.442	0.3246
21	Bombay cycle	0.388	0.41	0.432	0.126	0.183	0.3078
22	Mishka Exim	0.238	0.502	0.42	0.307	0.465	0.3864
23	ABans enetrpris	0.22	0.19	0.222	0.21	0.607	0.2898
24	Starlite compo	0.49	0.468	0.476	0.503	0.557	0.4988
25	CCL int.	0.367	0.347	0.477	0.402	0.464	0.4114
26	WH brady	0.421	0.449	0.548	0.601	0.65	0.5338
27	Maximaa Systems	0.059	0.024	-0.061	-0.105	-0.284	-0.0734
28	Mystic Electr	0.232	0.293	0.334	0.328	0.354	0.3082
29	Gayatri bio	0.166	0.263	0.215	0.206	0.335	0.237
30	Empower India	0.383	0.351	0.36	0.319	-0.113	0.26
	Average	0.3532	0.369333	0.373133	0.3538670	386567	

(SOURCE – WWW.MONEYCONTROL.COM AND EXCEL)

F-Test (ANOVA) Analysis:

The researcher has applied the two-way analysis of variance (F-Test) to judge the significance variance in company - wise and year-wise net working capital ratio of sampled companies working as Trading Houses in India. Abstract of F-Test is shown in table 4.14.The summary of the results of the analysis of variance test is shown in table - 4.15

Table - 4.14
Abstract of F-Test

SR. NO	SUMMARY	Count	Sum	Average	Variance
1	Adani eneterpris	5	2.021	0.4042	0.055088
2	MMTC ltd	5	2.692	0.5384	0.011087
3	PTC India	5	1.955	0.391	0.004711
4	Swan energy	5	1.235	0.247	0.012944
5	Andrew yule	5	4.783	0.9566	0.000328
6	STC India	5	4.25	0.85	0.000101
7	Shaily India	5	1.755	0.351	0.004654
8	Ind motor parts	5	1.504	0.3008	0.005237
9	Uniphos Ent	5	3.821	0.7642	0.00024
10	Grandeur Prod	5	4.29	0.858	0.000336
11	Control print	5	2.492	0.4984	0.003579
12	Apollo Tricoat	5	2.104	0.4208	0.021956
13	Sat Ind	5	2.248	0.4496	0.01224
14	Singer India	5	1.259	0.2518	0.001666
15	Urja Global	5	-0.014	-0.0028	0.000582
16	Competent Auto	5	0.214	0.0428	0.001125
17	High Ground Ent	5	0.204	0.0408	0.003888
18	Cravatex	5	-1.052	-0.2104	0.00322
19	Lahoti Over	5	1.9	0.38	0.007644
20	Tandl Global	5	1.623	0.3246	0.007798
21	Bombay cycle	5	1.539	0.3078	0.020232
22	Mishka Exim	5	1.932	0.3864	0.012249
23	ABans enetrpris	5	1.449	0.2898	0.031603
24	Starlite compo	5	2.494	0.4988	0.001238
25	CCL int.	5	2.057	0.4114	0.003319
26	WH brady	5	2.669	0.5338	0.009534
27	Maximaa Systems	5	-0.367	-0.0734	0.01813
28	Mystic Electr	5	1.541	0.3082	0.002298
29	Gayatri bio	5	1.185	0.237	0.004192
30	Empower India	5	1.3	0.26	0.044005

Year-2011-2012	30	10.596	0.3532	0.07168
Year-2012-2013	30	11.194	0.373133	0.068853
Year-2013-2014	30	11.08	0.369333	0.079538
Year-2014-2015	30	10.616	0.353887	0.079156
Year-2015-2016	30	11.597	0.386567	0.093226

(SOURCE – WWW.MONEYCONTROL.COM AND EXCEL)

Table - 4.15

Result of F-Test

Source of Variation	SS	DF	MSS	F-Cal. Value	5% F Limit
Companies	10.1839	28	0.351169	34.02463	1.565322
Years	0.023658	4	0.005914	0.573053	2.44988
Error	1.197239	116	0.010321		
Total	11.4048	149			

(SOURCE – WWW.MONEYCONTROL.COM AND EXCEL)

From the Table- 4.15 it is observed that:

H_1 Calculated F-Value is statistically greater than the F-Table Value at 5% significance level. Therefore the result of the F-Test rejects the null hypothesis. So we conclude that there is significant variation among company-wise net working capital ratio of sampled companies working as Trading Houses in India.

H_0 F-Calculated value is less than F-Table value. Therefore, the result of the F-Test accepts the null hypothesis. So we conclude that there is **no** significant variation among year-wise net working capital ratio of sampled companies working as Trading Houses in India.

❖ **INVENTORY TURNOVER:**

This ratio indicates the efficiency of the sampled Trading Houses in selling its product. It is calculated by dividing the sale by inventory.

$$\text{Inventory Turnover} = \frac{\text{Sales}}{\text{Inventory}}$$

The inventory turnover shows how rapidly the inventory is turning in to receivable through sales. Generally, a high inventory turnover is indicative of good inventory management. A low inventory turnover implies excessive inventory levels than warranted by production and sales activities, or a slow-moving or obsolete inventor

A high level of sluggish inventory amounts to unnecessary tie-up of funds reduced profit and increased costs. If the obsolete inventories have to be written off, this will adversely affect the working capital and liquidity position of the firm. Again, a relatively high inventory turnover should be carefully analyzed. A high inventory turnover may be the result of a very low level of inventory which results in frequent stock outs; the firm may be living from hand to mouth. The turnover will also be high if the firm replenishes its inventory in too many small lot sizes. The situations of frequents stockouts and too many small inventory replacements are costly for the firm. Thus, high and too low inventory turnover ratios should be investigate further. The computation of inventory turnovers for individual components of inventory may help to detect the imbalanced investments in the various inventory components.

The researcher has examined inventory turnover ratio of 30 Trading houses for the period of 2011-2012 to 2015-16. The summaries of inventory turnover ratio of selected trading houses are as follows:

The following table 4.16 indicates inventory turnover ratio of sampled companies working as trading houses in India for the period of 2011-2012 to 2015-16.

Table - 4.16

Inventory Turnover Ratio of Sampled Trading Houses

SR. NO	Trading Houses	2011-12	2012-13	2013-14	2014-15	2015-16	Average
1	Adani eneterpris	35	44	71	42	63	51
2	MMTC ltd	20	22	49	36	42	33.8
3	PTC India	51	53	46	52	53	51
4	Swan energy	99	111	97	114	146	113.4
5	Andrew yule	84	75	73	103	82	83.4
6	STC India	144	180	141	149	173	157.4
7	Shaily India	157	150	92	115	135	129.8
8	Ind motor parts	76	77	88	82	148	94.2
9	Uniphos Ent	140	99	140	218	188	157
10	Grandeur Prod	221	183	151	193	202	190
11	Control print	112	148	111	123	119	122.6
12	Apollo Tricoat	68	70	62	56	56	62.4
13	Sat Ind	60	54	68	77	70	65.8
14	Singer India	143	178	143	209	181	170.8
15	Urja Global	19	20	19	21	26	21
16	Competent Auto	54	55	51	67	52	55.8
17	High Ground Ent	24	39	32	42	54	38.2
18	Cravatex	55	48	42	47	52	48.8
19	Lahoti Over	107	104	119	76	89	99
20	Tandl Global	75	85	68	71	76	75
21	Bombay cycle	32	47	65	103	111	71.6
22	Mishka Exim	31	84	57	61	74	61.4
23	ABans enetrpris	103	94	95	76	101	93.8
24	Starlite compo	110	88	100	108	108	102.8
25	CCL int.	106	133	134	103	108	116.8
26	WH brady	83	78	79	78	90	81.6
27	Maximaa Systems	73	94	93	65	24	69.8
28	Mystic Electr	60	80	55	58	49	60.4
29	Gayatri bio	37	49	50	53	58	49.4
30	Empower India	44	52	44	40	38	43.6
	Average	87.93333	80.76667	81.16667	87.93333	2.26667	

(SOURCE – WWW.MONEYCONTROL.COM AND EXCEL)

F-Test (ANOVA) Analysis:

The researcher has applied the two-way analysis of variance (F-Test) to judge the significance variance in company - wise and year-wise inventory turnover ratio of sampled companies working as Trading Houses in India. Abstract of F-Test is shown in table 4.17

Table - 4.17 Abstract of F-Test

SR NO	SUMMARY	Count	Sum	Average	Variance
1	Adani eneterpris	5	37.68	7.536	4.54288
2	MMTC ltd	5	60.59	12.118	24.33447
3	PTC India	5	35.33	7.066	0.19063
4	Swan energy	5	16.22	3.244	0.24788
5	Andrew yule	5	21.89	4.378	0.33247
6	STC India	5	11.55	2.31	0.0644
7	Shaily India	5	14.37	2.874	0.43118
8	Ind motor parts	5	20.25	4.05	0.87135
9	Uniphos Ent	5	12.34	2.468	0.58842
10	Grandeur Prod	5	9.63	1.928	0.08213
11	Control print	5	14.81	2.962	0.10537
12	Apollo Tricoat	5	29.08	5.816	0.37808
13	Sat Ind	5	27.72	5.544	0.58923
14	Singer India	5	10.77	2.154	0.12528
15	Urja Global	5	88.88	17.336	4.79443
16	Competent Auto	5	32.61	6.522	0.46092
17	High Ground Ent	5	50.87	10.174	10.78743
18	Cravatex	5	37.37	7.474	0.59388
19	Lahoti Over	5	18.61	3.722	0.43387
20	Tandl Global	5	24.15	4.83	0.16175
21	Bombay cycle	5	31.29	6.258	11.15857
22	Mishka Exim	5	33.07	6.614	8.82343
23	ABans enetrpris	5	19.33	3.866	0.24763
24	Starlite compo	5	17.86	3.532	0.11902
25	CCL int.	5	15.59	3.118	0.15682
26	WH brady	5	22.09	4.418	0.06952
27	Maximaa Systems	5	33.17	6.634	22.42393
28	Mystic Electr	5	30.64	6.128	1.08477
29	Gayatri bio	5	37.38	7.476	1.74958
30	Empower India	5	41.78	8.356	1.01303
	Year-2011-2012	30	195.55	6.518333	20.76332
	Year-2012-2013	30	168.93	5.631	13.89668
	Year-2013-2014	30	188.02	5.600867	11.29737
	Year-2014-2015	30	163.31	5.443667	10.19447
	Year-2015-2016	30	158.71	5.290333	10.39247

Table - 4.18 Result of F-Test

Source of Variation	SS	DF	MSS	F-Cal. Value	5% F Limit
Companies	1569.476864	29	54.11989	17.42372	1.585322
Years	27.53339733	4	6.883349	2.216072	2.44988
Error	360.3080027	116	3.106103		
Total	1957.318264	149			

(SOURCE – WWW.MONEYCONTROL.COM AND EXCEL)

From the Table- 4.18 it is observed that:

H_1 Calculated F-Value is statistically greater than the F-Table Value at 5% significance level. Therefore the result of the F-Test rejects the null hypothesis. So we conclude that there is significant variation among company-wise inventory turnover ratio of sampled companies working as Trading Houses in India.

H_0 F-Calculated value is statistically less than F-Table value at 5% significance level. Therefore, the result of the F-Test accepts the null hypothesis. So we conclude that there is no significant variation among year-wise inventory turnover ratio of sampled companies working as Trading Houses in India.

❖ **INVENTORY TO WORKING CAPITAL RATIO :**

This ratio establishes a relationship between inventory and net current assets of sampled Trading Houses in India. This ratio shows the extent of inventories in current assets of sampled companies under study. Inventory to working capital ratio is calculated as per follows:

$$\text{Inventory To Working Capital Ratio} = \frac{\text{Inventory}}{\text{Net Current Assets}}$$

The researcher has examined inventory to working capital ratio of 30 Trading houses for the period of 2011-2012 to 2015-16. The summary of inventory to working capital ratio of selected trading houses is as follows:

The following table 4.19 indicates inventory to working capital ratio of sampled companies working as Trading Houses in India for the period of 2011-2012 to 2015-16.

Table - 4.19

Inventory to Working Capital Ratio of Sampled Trading Houses

SR.NO.	Trading Houses	2011-12	2012-13	2013-14	2014-15	2015-16	Average
1	Adani eneterpris	0.7	0.89	0.8	0.72	0.91	0.804
2	MMTC ltd	0.98	0.95	0.67	0.56	1.04	0.84
3	PTC India	0.96	0.72	0.6	0.7	1.09	0.814
4	Swan energy	0.91	1.52	1.38	0.76	0.57	1.028
5	Andrew yule	0.33	0.31	0.31	0.39	0.34	0.336
6	STC India	0.6	0.66	0.55	0.64	0.66	0.622
7	Shaily India	0.92	0.76	0.69	0.67	0.48	0.704
8	Ind motor parts	0.63	0.85	0.54	0.73	0.5	0.65
9	Uniphos Ent	0.88	0.79	0.77	0.86	0.83	0.826
10	Grandeur Prod	0.89	0.8	0.79	0.86	0.76	0.82
11	Control print	0.82	0.92	0.82	0.84	0.74	0.828
12	Apollo Tricoat	0.63	0.48	0.73	0.12	0.14	0.42
13	Sat Ind	0.29	0.26	0.76	0.81	0.35	0.494
14	Singer India	0.75	1.29	0.99	1.13	0.78	0.988
15	Urja Global	1.21	-0.1	1.5	-1.95	-0.7	-0.008
16	Competent Auto	1.09	1.37	4.5	4.44	11.81	4.642
17	High Ground Ent	0.71	1.17	0.83	-37.64	-2.91	-7.568
18	Cravatex	-0.78	-0.86	-0.54	-0.95	-1.13	-0.852
19	Lahoti Over	0.73	0.79	0.94	0.75	0.8	0.802
20	Tandl Global	0.82	1.02	1.01	0.75	0.47	0.814
21	Bombay cycle	0.15	0.21	0.3	1.06	0.76	0.496
22	Mishka Exim	0.48	0.82	0.77	0.79	0.64	0.7
23	ABans enetrpris	0.71	0.69	0.55	0.4	0.11	0.492
24	Starlite compo	0.7	0.75	0.88	0.88	0.78	0.798
25	CCL int.	0.71	0.97	0.82	0.85	0.59	0.788
26	WH brady	0.67	0.6	0.5	0.44	0.48	0.538
27	Maximaa Systems	2.8	11.63	-4.8	-2.59	-0.36	1.336
28	Mystic Electr	0.83	0.9	0.71	0.6	0.51	0.71
29	Gayatri bio	1.48	1.17	1.22	1.42	0.9	1.238
30	Empower India	0.32	0.45	0.43	0.48	-2.1	-0.084
	Average		0.764	1.092667	0.667333	-0.68267	0.661333

(SOURCE – WWW.MONEYCONTROL.COM AND EXCEL)

F-Test (ANOVA) Analysis:

The researcher has applied the two-way analysis of variance (F-Test) to judge the significance variance in company - wise and year-wise inventory to working capital ratio of sampled companies working as Trading Houses in India. Abstract of F-Test is shown in table 4.20.

Table - 4.20
Abstract of F-Test

SR.NO	SUMMARY	Count	Sum	Average	Variance
1	Adani eneterpris	5	4.02	0.804	0.00913
2	MMTC ltd	5	4.2	0.84	0.04475
3	PTC India	5	4.07	0.814	0.04128
4	Swan energy	5	5.14	1.028	0.16537
5	Andrew Yule	5	1.88	0.338	0.00108
6	STC India	5	3.11	0.622	0.00222
7	Shaily India	5	3.52	0.704	0.02533
8	Ind motor parts	5	3.25	0.85	0.02035
9	Uniphos Ent	5	4.13	0.826	0.00213
10	Grandeur Prod	5	4.1	0.82	0.00285
11	Control print	5	4.14	0.828	0.00412
12	Apollo Tricoat	5	2.1	0.42	0.07805
13	Sat Ind	5	2.47	0.494	0.07193
14	Singer India	5	4.94	0.988	0.05282
15	Urja Global	5	-0.04	-0.008	2.00407
16	Competent Auto	5	23.21	4.642	18.69097
17	High Ground Ent	5	-37.84	-7.588	285.3566
18	Cravatex	5	-4.26	-0.852	0.04737
19	Lahoti Over	5	4.01	0.802	0.00677
20	Tandl Global	5	4.07	0.814	0.05083
21	Bombay cycle	5	2.48	0.496	0.15693
22	Mishka Exim	5	3.5	0.7	0.01985
23	ABans enetrpris	5	2.46	0.492	0.08112
24	Starlite compo	5	3.99	0.798	0.00842
25	CCL int.	5	3.94	0.788	0.02082
26	WH brady	5	2.69	0.538	0.00892
27	Maximaa Systems	5	6.68	1.336	41.01253
28	Mystic Electr	5	3.55	0.71	0.02585
29	Gayatri bio	5	8.19	1.238	0.05272
30	Empower India	5	-0.42	-0.034	1.27373
	Year-2011-2012	30	22.92	0.764	0.299158
	Year-2012-2013	30	32.78	1.092667	4.171186
	Year-2013-2014	30	20.02	0.687333	1.869772
	Year-2014-2015	30	-20.48	-0.68267	49.95933
	Year-2015-2016	30	19.84	0.681333	5.25055

(SOURCE – WWW.MONEYCONTROL.COM AND EXCEL)

The summary of the results of the analysis of variance test is shown in table - 4.21

Table - 4.21

Result of F-Test

Source of Variation	SS	DF	MSS	F-Cal. Value	5% F Limit
Companies	438.0932	29	15.10866	1.306711	1.565322
Years	56.21033	4	14.05258	1.215534	2.44988
Error	1341.057	116	11.56083		
Total	1835.36	149			

(SOURCE – WWW.MONEYCONTROL.COM AND EXCEL)

From the Table- 4.21 it is observed that:

H_0 Calculated F-Value is statistically less than the F-Table Value at 5% significance level. Therefore, the result of the F-Test accepts the null hypothesis. So we conclude that there is no significant variation among company-wise inventory to working capital ratio of sampled companies working as Trading Houses in India.

H_1 Calculated F-Value is statistically less than the F-Table Value at 5% significance level. Therefore, the result of the F-Test accepts the null hypothesis. So we conclude that there is no significant variation among year-wise inventory to working capital ratio of sampled companies working as Trading Houses in India.

❖ **DEBTORS TURNOVER:**

A firm sells goods for cash and Credit is used as a marketing tool by a number of companies. When the firm extends credits to its customers, book debts (debtors or receivables) are created in the firm's accounts. Book debts are axpected to be converted into cash over a short period and, therefore, are included in current assets. Debtor's turnover can be calculated by dividing total sales by the year-end balance of debtors:

$$\text{Debtors Turnover} = \frac{\text{Sales}}{\text{Debtors}}$$

The researcher has examined debtors turnover ratio of 30 Trading houses for the period of 2011-2012 to 2015-16. The summaries of debtor's turnover ratio of selected trading houses are as follows:

The following table 4.22 indicates debtor's turnover ratio of sampled companies working as trading houses in India for the period of 2011-2012 to 2015-16.

Table - 4.22

Debtors Turnover Ratio of Sampled Trading Houses

SR. NO	Trading Houses	2011-12	2012-13	2013-14	2014-15	2015-16	Average
1	Adani eneterpris	22	23	26	20	18	21.8
2	MMTC ltd	46	43	48	46	32	43
3	PTC India	84	76	69	68	61	71.6
4	Swan energy	17	15	32	81	70	43
5	Andrew yule	160	145	148	146	143	148.4
6	STC India	110	110	106	98	132	111.2
7	Shaily India	86	129	109	118	85	105.4
8	Ind motor parts	75	60	90	85	85	79
9	Uniphos Ent	35	31	33	63	71	46.6
10	Grandeur Prod	34	39	26	39	41	35.8
11	Control print	72	89	98	70	109	87.6
12	Apollo Tricoat	56	90	49	70	55	64
13	Sat Ind	136	154	68	73	79	102
14	Singer India	114	58	78	105	136	98.2
15	Urja Global	5	6	11	6	19	9.4
16	Competent Auto	6	7	10	12	8	8.6
17	High Ground Ent	41	37	60	15	14	33.4
18	Cravatex	58	39	22	14	13	29.2
19	Lahoti Over	61	57	52	56	61	57.4
20	Tandl Global	38	23	26	26	57	34
21	Bombay cycle	70	55	36	28	24	42.6
22	Mishka Exim	30	53	54	36	34	41.4
23	ABans enetrpris	39	61	58	60	73	58.2
24	Starlite compo	59	36	27	34	40	39.2
25	CCL int.	46	41	44	41	42	42.8
26	WH brady	100	108	111	116	115	110
27	Maximaa Systems	19	18	15	18	13	16.6
28	Mystic Electr	42	33	29	31	42	35.4
29	Gayatri bio	44	17	23	25	24	26.6
30	Empower India	60	56	63	55	53	57.4
	Average	58.83333	56.96667	54.03333	55.16667	58.3	

(SOURCE – WWW.MONEYCONTROL.COM AND EXCEL)

F-Test (ANOVA) Analysis:

The researcher has applied the two-way analysis of variance (F-Test) to judge the significance variance in company - wise and year-wise debtors turnover ratio of sampled companies working as Trading Houses in India. Abstract of F-Test is shown in table 4.23.

Table - 4.23 Abstract of F-Test

SR.NO	SUMMARY	Count	Sum	Average	Variance
1	Adani Enterprise	5	83.48	16.696	5.03073
2	MMTC ltd	5	42.7	8.54	2.47185
3	PTC India	5	25.43	5.086	0.38793
4	Swan energy	5	66.38	13.276	83.00173
5	Andrew Yule	5	12.16	2.432	0.01257
6	STC India	5	16.38	3.278	0.12283
7	Shaily India	5	15.98	3.198	0.37653
8	Ind motor parts	5	23.17	4.634	0.59778
9	Uniphos Ent	5	43.85	8.77	9.75525
10	Grandeur Prod	5	51.4	10.28	4.54205
11	Control print	5	19.74	3.948	0.41457
12	Apollo Tricoat	5	29.5	5.9	1.74535
13	Sat Ind	5	19.76	3.952	1.87237
14	Singer India	5	20.04	4.008	2.00392
15	Urja Global	5	239.73	47.946	519.4293
16	Competent Auto	5	228.28	45.852	167.1093
17	High Ground Ent	5	73.91	14.782	85.60907
18	Cravatex	5	84.72	16.944	90.94048
19	Lahoti Over	5	31.41	6.282	0.21062
20	Tandl Global	5	59.35	11.87	14.9546
21	Bombay cycle	5	49.88	9.978	17.74523
22	Mishka Exim	5	48.13	9.226	5.65268
23	ABans enetrpris	5	32.03	6.406	2.41318
24	Starlite compo	5	49.04	9.808	7.18447
25	CCL int.	5	42.08	8.412	0.17217
26	WH brady	5	16.37	3.274	0.04093
27	Maximaa Systems	5	111.14	22.228	13.62827
28	Mystic Electr	5	52.29	10.458	3.10277
29	Gayatri bio	5	74.83	14.966	23.00138
30	Empower India	5	31.48	6.296	0.21173
	Year-2011-2012	30	354.7	11.82333	260.0629
	Year-2012-2013	30	362.9	12.09667	194.4561
	Year-2013-2014	30	315.88	10.52933	68.99521
	Year-2014-2015	30	331.8	11.06	99.21699
	Year-2015-2016	30	327.32	10.91067	106.0826

(SOURCE – WWW.MONEYCONTROL.COM AND EXCEL)

The summary of the results of the analysis of variance test is shown in table - 4.24

Table - 4.24 Result of F-Test

Source of Variation	SS	DF	MSS	F-Cal. Value	5% F Limit
Companies	16931.37	29	583.8402	18.11109	1.565322
Years	51.31149	4	12.82787	0.353986	2.44988
Error	4203.655	116	36.23841		
Total	21186.33	149			

(SOURCE – WWW.MONEYCONTROL.COM AND EXCEL)

From the Table- 4.24 it is observed that:

H_1 — Calculated F-Value is statistically greater than the F-Table Value at 5% significance level. Therefore the result of the F-Test rejects the null hypothesis. So we conclude that there is significant variation among company-wise debtors turnover ratio of sampled companies working as Trading Houses in India.

H_0 — F-Calculated value is statistically less than F-Table value at 5% significance level. Therefore, the result of the F-Test accepts the null hypothesis. So we conclude that there is no significant variation among year-wise debtors turnover ratio of sampled companies working as Trading Houses in India.

❖ AVERAGE COLLECTION PERIOD:

The average number of days for which books debts remain outstanding is called the average collection period (ACP) and can be computed as follows :

$$ACP = \frac{Debtors * 360}{Sales}$$

The average collection period measures the quality of debtors since it indicates the speed of their collection. The shorter the average collection period, the better the quality of debtors, as a short collection period implies the prompt payments by debtors the average collection Period should be compared against the firm's credit terms and policy to judge its credit and collection efficiency.

The researcher has examined average collection period of 30 Trading houses for the period of 2011-2012 to 2015-16. The summaries of average collection period of selected Trading Houses are as follows:

The following table 4.25 indicates average collection period of sampled companies working as Trading Houses in India for the period of 2011-2012 to 2015-16.

Table - 4.25
Average Collection Period of Sampled Trading Houses

SR.NO.	Trading Houses	2011-12	2012-13	2013-14	2014-15	2015-16	Average
1	Adani eneterpris	22	23	26	20	18	21.8
2	MMTC ltd	46	43	48	46	32	43
3	PTC India	84	76	68	68	61	71.4
4	Swan energy	17	15	32	81	70	43
5	Andrew yule	160	145	148	144	142	147.8
6	STC India	110	110	106	97	131	110.8
7	Shaily India	86	129	109	118	135	115.4
8	Ind motor parts	75	61	90	85	85	79.2
9	Uniphos Ent	35	31	33	63	71	46.6
10	Grandeur Prod	34	39	26	39	41	35.8
11	Control print	72	89	97	97	109	92.8
12	Apollo Tricoat	56	89	49	70	55	63.8
13	Sat Ind	136	154	68	73	79	102
14	Singer India	113	58	78	105	136	98
15	Urja Global	5	6	11	8	19	9.8
16	Competent Auto	30	25	17	12	18	20.4
17	High Ground Ent	41	37	61	15	14	33.6
18	Cravatex	58	40	22	14	13	29.4
19	Lahoti Over	61	57	52	56	61	57.4
20	Tandl Global	38	23	26	26	57	34
21	Bombay cycle	70	55	36	28	24	42.6
22	Mishka Exim	30	53	54	34	34	41
23	ABans enetrpris	40	61	58	60	73	58.4
24	Starlite compo	59	36	27	34	40	39.2
25	CCL int.	46	41	44	41	42	42.8
26	WH brady	100	108	111	116	115	110
27	Maximaa Systems	19	18	158	18	13	45.2
28	Mystic Electr	41	33	29	31	43	35.4
29	Gayatri bio	44	17	23	25	24	26.6
30	Empower India	60	56	63	56	52	57.4
	Average	59.6	57.6	59	566	0.23333	

(SOURCE – WWW.MONEYCONTROL.COM AND EXCEL)

F-Test (ANOVA) Analysis:

The researcher has applied the two-way analysis of variance (F-Test) to judge the significance variance in company - wise and year-wise average collection period of sampled companies working as Trading Houses in India. Abstract of F-Test is shown in table 4.26.

Table - 4.26 Abstract of F-Test

SR.NO	SUMMARY	Count	Sum	Average	Variance
1	Adani eneterpris	5	109	21.8	9.2
2	MMTC ltd	5	215	43	41
3	PTC India	5	357	71.4	77.8
4	Swan energy	5	215	43	938.5
5	Andrew yule	5	739	147.8	51.2
6	STC India	5	554	110.8	155.7
7	Shaily India	5	577	115.4	370.3
8	Ind motor parts	5	396	79.2	133.2
9	Uniphos Ent	5	233	46.6	356.8
10	Grandeur Prod	5	179	35.8	36.7
11	Control print	5	464	92.8	186.2
12	Apollo Tricoat	5	319	83.8	257.7
13	Sat Ind	5	510	102	1596.5
14	Singer India	5	490	98	929.5
15	Urja Global	5	49	9.8	31.7
16	Competent Auto	5	102	20.4	50.3
17	High Ground Ent	5	168	33.6	386.8
18	Cravatex	5	147	29.4	372.8
19	Lahoti Over	5	287	57.4	14.3
20	Tandl Global	5	170	34	198.5
21	Bombay cycle	5	213	42.6	376.8
22	Mishka Exim	5	205	41	133
23	ABans enetrpris	5	292	58.4	140.3
24	Starlite compo	5	196	39.2	144.7
25	CCL int.	5	214	42.8	4.7
26	WH brady	5	550	110	41.5
27	Maximaa Systems	5	83	16.6	6.3
28	Mystic Electr	5	177	35.4	38.8
29	Gayatri bio	5	133	26.6	104.3
30	Empower India	5	287	57.4	17.8
	Year-2011-2012	30	1788	59.6	1302.662
	Year-2012-2013	30	1728	57.6	1523.421
	Year-2013-2014	30	1627	54.23333	1169.495
	Year-2014-2015	30	1680	56	1323.724
	Year-2015-2016	30	1807	60.23333	1628.806

(SOURCE – WWW.MONEYCONTROL.COM AND EXCEL)

The summary of the results of the analysis of variance test is shown in table - 4.27

Table - 4.27
Result of F-Test

Source of Variation	SS	DF	MSS	F-Cal. Value	5% F Limit
Companies	173427.7	29	5980.267	24.7159	1.565322
Years	744.2	4	186.05	0.768928	2.44988
Error	28067.4	116	241.9603		
Total	202239.3	149			

(SOURCE – WWW.MONEYCONTROL.COM AND EXCEL)

From the Table- 4.27 it is observed that:

H_1 Calculated F-Value is statistically greater than the F-Table Value at 5% significance level. Therefore the result of the F-Test rejects the null hypothesis. So we conclude that there is significant variation among company-wise average collection period of sampled companies working as Trading Houses in India.

H_0 F-Calculated value is statistically less than F-Table value at 5% significance level. Therefore, the result of the F-Test accepts the null hypothesis. So we conclude that there is no significant variation among year-wise average collection period of sampled companies working as Trading Houses in India.

❖ CURRENT ASSETS TURNOVER:

This ratio establishes a relationship between sales and current assets of sampled companies working as Trading Houses in India. This also indicates the extent at which current assets of sampled Trading Houses generate sales. This ratio is calculated as per following way :

Hypothesis Testing:

$$\text{Current Assets Turnover Ratio} = \frac{\text{Sales}}{\text{Current Assets}}$$

The researcher has examined current assets turnover ratio of 30 Trading houses for the period of 2011-2012 to 2015-16. The summaries of current assets turnover ratio of selected trading houses are as follows:

The following table 4.28 indicates current assets turnover ratio of sampled companies working as Trading Houses in India for the period of 2011-2012 to 2015-16.

Table - 4.28
Current Assets Turnover Ratio of Sampled Trading Houses

SR.NO	Trading Houses	2011-12	2012-13	2013-14	2014-15	2015-16	Average
1	Adani eneterpris	4.7	4.57	3.39	4.21	4.29	4.232
2	MMTC ltd	4.31	4.41	2.3	2.62	3.09	3.346
3	PTC India	2.04	2.09	1.83	1.83	2.28	2.014
4	Swan energy	1.95	1.93	1.86	1.33	1	1.614
5	Andrew yule	1.33	1.44	1.41	1.27	1.34	1.358
6	STC India	0.75	1.13	1.24	1.31	1.06	1.098
7	Shaily India	1.24	1.1	1.49	1.21	0.86	1.18
8	Ind motor parts	1.76	1.99	1.3	1.5	0.89	1.488
9	Uniphos Ent	1.92	2.44	1.8	1.21	1.19	1.712
10	Grandeur Prod	1.3	1.48	1.73	1.38	1.2	1.418
11	Control print	1.31	1.11	1.28	1.25	1.26	1.242
12	Apollo Tricoat	2.13	1.62	1.94	0.68	0.74	1.422
13	Sat Ind	1.11	1.09	1.77	1.7	1.17	1.368
14	Singer India	1.08	1.21	1.33	0.92	0.92	1.092
15	Urja Global	3.47	4.36	3.68	4.33	2.22	3.612
16	Competent Auto	2.19	2.12	2.7	2.62	3.09	2.544
17	High Ground Ent	1.96	2.38	2.07	3.23	2.04	2.336
18	Cravatex	2.01	1.94	2.92	2.98	2.18	2.406
19	Lahoti Over	1.62	1.68	1.62	1.93	1.72	1.714
20	Tandl Global	1.59	1.97	2.43	2.5	1.74	2.046
21	Bombay cycle	1	1.11	1.19	1.29	1.37	1.192
22	Mishka Exim	2.9	1.92	2.62	2.24	1.75	2.286
23	ABans enetrpris	1.68	1.47	1.27	1.25	0.35	1.204
24	Starlite compo	1.65	2.19	2.03	1.94	1.8	1.922
25	CCL int.	1.51	1.48	1.51	1.79	1.3	1.518
26	WH brady	1.66	1.62	1.46	1.4	1.37	1.502
27	Maximaa Systems	1.89	1.9	2.3	3.03	4.9	2.804
28	Mystic Electr	2.82	2.55	3.07	2.68	2.66	2.756
29	Gayatri bio	2.48	2.43	2.33	2.47	2.16	2.374
30	Empower India	1.27	1.32	1.38	1.54	3.08	1.718
	Average	1.954333	2.001667	1.975	1.988	1.834	

(SOURCE – WWW.MONEYCONTROL.COM AND EXCEL)

F-Test (ANOVA) Analysis:

The researcher has applied the two-way analysis of variance (F-Test) to judge the significance variance in company - wise and year-wise current assets turnover ratio of sampled companies working as Trading Houses in India. Abstract of F-Test is shown in table 4.29. The summary of the results of the analysis of variance test is shown in table - 4.30

Table - 4.29 Abstract of F-Test

SR.NO	SUMMARY	Count	Sum	Average	Variance
1	Adani eneterpris	5	21.16	4.232	0.26152
2	MMTC ltd	5	16.73	3.346	0.93703
3	PTC India	5	10.07	2.014	0.03623
4	Swan energy	5	8,07	1.614	0.18273
5	Andrew yule	5	6.79	1.358	0.00457
6	STC India	5	5.49	1.098	0.04717
7	Shaily India	5	5.9	1.18	0.05235
8	Ind motor parts	5	7.44	1.488	0.17977
9	Uniphos Ent	5	3.56	1.712	0.27637
10	Grandeur Prod	5	7.09	1.418	0.04102
11	Control print	5	6.21	1.242	0.00597
12	Apollo Tricoat	5	7.11	1.422	0.45612
13	Sat Ind	5	6.84	1.368	0.11372
14	Singer India	5	5.46	1.092	0.03247
15	Urja Global	5	18.08	3.612	0.75937
16	Competent Auto	5	12.72	2.544	0.15833
17	High Ground Ent	5	11.88	2.338	0.27523
18	Cravatex	5	12.03	2.406	0.25468
19	Lahoti Over	5	8.57	1.714	0.01638
20	Tandl Global	5	10.23	2.048	0.16523
21	Bombay cycle	5	5.96	1.192	0.02122
22	Mishka Exim	5	11.43	2.288	0.22798
23	ABans enetrpris	5	6.02	1.204	0.25828
24	Starlite compo	5	9.61	1.922	0.04317
25	CCL int.	5	7.59	1.518	0.03077
26	WH brady	5	7.51	1.502	0.01712
27	Maximaa Systems	5	14.02	2.804	1.58773
28	Mystic Electr	5	13.78	2.756	0.04003
29	Gayatri bio	5	11.87	2.374	0.01783
30	Empower India	5	8.43	1.686	0.60938
	Year-2011-2012	30	58.63	1.954333	0.834198
	Year-2012-2013	30	60.05	2.001687	0.87878
	Year-2013-2014	30	59.25	1.975	0.454881
	Year-2014-2015	30	59.48	1.982667	0.84111
	Year-2015-2016	30	55.02	1.834	1.082218

(SOURCE – WWW.MONEYCONTROL.COM AND EXCEL)

Table - 4.30 Result of F-Test

Source of Variation	SS	DF	MSS	F-Cal. Value	5% F Limit
Companies	90.74039	29	3.128979	13.0075	1.565322
Years	0.535057	4	0.133764	0.556073	2.44988
Error	27.90402	116	0.240552		
Total	119.1795	149			

(SOURCE – WWW.MONEYCONTROL.COM AND EXCEL)

From the Table- 4.30 it is observed that:

H_1 Calculated F-Value is statistically greater than the F-Table Value at 5% significance level. Therefore the result of the F-Test rejects the null hypothesis. So we conclude that there is significant variation among company-wise current assets turnover ratio of sampled companies working as Trading Houses in India.

H_0 F-Calculated value is statistically less than F-Table value at 5% significance level. Therefore, the result of the F-Test accepts the null hypothesis. So we conclude that there is no significant variation among year-wise current assets turnover ratio of sampled companies working as Trading Houses in India.

❖ **WORKING CAPITAL TURNOVER RATIO:**

This ratio establishes a relationship between sales and net working capital of sampled companies working as Trading Houses in India. This ratio is calculated as follows:

$$\text{Working capital turnover ration} = \frac{\text{sales}}{\text{Net working capital}}$$

The researcher has examined working capital turnover ratio of 30 Trading houses for the period of 2011-2012 to 2015-16. The summaries of working capital turnover ratio of selected trading houses are as follows:

The following table 4.31 indicates working capital turnover ratio of sampled companies working as Trading Houses in India for the period of 2011-2012 to 2015-16.

Table - 4.31

Working Capital Turnover Ratio of Sampled Trading Houses

SR. NO	Trading Houses	2011-12	2012-13	2013-14	2014-15	2015-16	Average
1	Adani eneterpris	7.16	7.21	4.06	6.32	5.21	5.992
2	MMTC ltd	18.01	15.92	4.98	5.55	8.99	10.69
3	PTC India	6.78	4.9	4.72	4.89	7.46	5.75
4	Swan energy	3.31	4.93	5.15	2.43	1.43	3.45
5	Andrew yule	1.44	1.52	1.53	1.37	1.49	1.47
6	STC India	1.52	1.32	1.41	1.55	1.38	1.436
7	Shaily India	2.12	1.83	2.71	2.1	1.28	2.008
8	Ind motor parts	3	3.97	2.23	3.21	1.22	2.726
9	Uniphos Ent	2.28	2.89	1.99	1.43	1.59	2.036
10	Grandeur Prod	1.46	1.57	1.89	1.6	1.36	1.576
11	Control print	2.65	2.25	2.66	2.47	2.25	2.456
12	Apollo Tricoat	3.35	2.47	4.3	0.83	0.9	2.37
13	Sat Ind	1.74	1.77	4.07	3.81	1.81	2.64
14	Singer India	1.89	2.61	2.51	1.94	1.57	2.104
15	Urja Global	22.58	-177.76	28.93	-34.12	-9.64	-34.002
16	Competent Auto	7.37	9.08	31.71	23.78	81.98	30.784
17	High Ground Ent	10.99	10.71	9.3	-321.61	-19.59	-62.04
18	Cravatex	-5.17	-6.33	-4.63	-7.39	-7.89	-6.282
19	Lahoti Over	2.5	2.76	2.87	3.55	3.24	2.984
20	Tandl Global	3.94	4.35	5.36	3.84	2.22	3.942
21	Bombay cycle	1.69	1.67	1.72	3.71	2.48	2.254
22	Mishka Exim	5.7	3.54	4.89	4.7	3.13	4.392
23	ABans enetrpris	2.48	2.64	2.09	1.89	0.4	1.9
24	Starlite compo	2.32	3.1	3.16	2.98	2.6	2.832
25	CCL int.	2.42	2.63	2.21	2.97	1.97	2.44
26	WH brady	2.96	2.79	2.29	2.06	1.93	2.406
27	Maximaa Systems	0.02	44.41	-18.58	-14.45	-5.46	1.188
28	Mystic Electr	5.02	4.1	4.71	3.76	3.79	4.276
29	Gayatri bio	14.41	8.72	8.94	9.66	5.62	9.47
30	Empower India	2.643	3.12	3.56	4.43	-20.01	-1.2514
	Average	4.619433	0.84367	4.424667	9.02467	2.823667	

(SOURCE – WWW.MONEYCONTROL.COM AND EXCEL)

F-Test (ANOVA) Analysis:

The researcher has applied the two-way analysis of variance (F-Test) to judge the significance variance in company - wise and year-wise working capital turnover ratio of sampled companies working as Trading Houses in India. Abstract of F-Test is shown in table 4.32.

Table - 4.32
Abstract of F-Test

SR.NO	SUMMARY	Count	Sum	Average	Variance
1	Adani eEnterprise	5	29.96	5.992	1.82487
2	MMTC ltd	5	53.45	10.69	35.71225
3	PTC India	5	28.75	5.75	1.627
4	Swan energy	5	17.25	3.45	2.5552
5	Andrew yule	5	7.35	1.47	0.00435
6	STC India	5	7.18	1.436	0.00933
7	Shaily India	5	10.04	2.008	0.26887
8	Ind motor parts	5	13.83	2.726	1.09273
9	Uniphos Ent	5	10.18	2.036	0.33928
10	Grandeur Prod	5	7.88	1.576	0.03983
11	Control print	5	12.28	2.456	0.04108
12	Apollo Tricoat	5	11.85	2.37	2.30695
13	Sat Ind	5	13.2	2.64	1.4174
14	Singer India	5	10.52	2.104	0.19468
15	Urja Global	5	-170.01	-34.002	7105.461
16	Competent Auto	5	153.92	30.784	922.5557
17	High Ground Ent	5	-310.2	-62.04	21223.48
18	Cravatex	5	-31.41	-8.282	1.94532
19	Lahoti Over	5	14.92	2.984	0.17083
20	Tandl Global	5	19.71	3.942	1.28822
21	Bombay cycle	5	11.27	2.254	0.77883
22	Mishka Exim	5	21.96	4.392	1.09307
23	ABans enetrpris	5	9.5	1.9	0.79255
24	Starlite compo	5	14.16	2.832	0.12932
25	CCL int.	5	12.2	2.44	0.1478
26	WH brady	5	12.03	2.406	0.20353
27	Maximaa Systems	5	5.94	1.188	637.2556
28	Mystic Electr	5	21.38	4.276	0.31883
29	Gayatri bio	5	47.35	9.47	10.0264
30	Empower India	5	-8.27	-1.254	110.3718
	Year-2011-2012	30	138.57	4.619	30.25059
	Year-2012-2013	30	-25.31	-0.84367	1185.217
	Year-2013-2014	30	132.74	4.424667	71.51988
	Year-2014-2015	30	-270.74	-9.02467	3563.716
	Year-2015-2016	30	84.71	2.823667	266.6014

(SOURCE – WWW.MONEYCONTROL.COM AND EXCEL)

The summary of the results of the analysis of variance test is shown in table - 4.33

Table - 4.33

Result of F-Test

Source of Variation	SS	DF	MSS	F-Cal. Value	5% F Limit
Companies	32055.31	29	1 105.355	1.102083	1.565322
Years	3907.293	4	976.8233	0.973914	2.44988
Error	116346.5	118	1002.987		
Total	152309.1	149			

(SOURCE – WWW.MONEYCONTROL.COM AND EXCEL)

From the Table- 4.33 it is observed that:

H_0 F-Calculated value is statistically less than F-Table value at 5% significance level. Therefore, the result of the F-Test accepts the null hypothesis. So we conclude that there is no significant variation among company-wise working capital turnover ratio of sampled companies working as Trading Houses in India.

H_1 F-Calculated value is statistically less than F-Table value at 5% significance level. Therefore, the result of the F-Test accepts the null hypothesis. So we conclude that there is no significant variation among year-wise working capital turnover ratio of sampled companies working as Trading Houses in India.

❖ **GROSS PROFIT MARGIN :**

Gross profit margin is calculated by dividing the gross profit by sales:

$$\text{Gross Profit Margin Ratio} = \frac{\text{Gross profit}}{\text{Sales}}$$

The gross profit margin reflects the efficiency with which management produces each unit of product. This ratio indicates the average spread between the cost of goods sold and the sales revenue. A high gross profit margin relative to the industry average implies that the firm is able to produce at relatively lower cost. A low gross profit margin may reflect higher cost of goods sold due to the firm's inability to purchase raw materials at favourable terms, inefficient utilization of plant and machinery, or over-investment in plant and machinery, resulting in higher cost of production. The ratio will also be low due to a fall in prices in the market, or marked reduction in selling prices by the firm in an attempt to obtain large sales volume, the cost of good sold remaining unchanged.

Table no 4.34
Gross profit margin ratio

SR. NO	Trading Houses	2011-12	2012-13	2013-14	2014-15	2015-16	Average
1	Adani eneterpris	0.02	0.04	0.04	0.04	0.05	0.038
2	MMTC ltd	0.01	0.01	0.02	0.02	0.02	0.016
3	PTC India	0.09	0.09	0.09	0.1	0.1	0.094
4	Swan energy	0.3	0.25	0.25	0.24	0.22	0.252
5	Andrew yule	0.03	0.03	0.02	0.03	0.03	0.028
6	STC India	0.03	0.03	0.03	0.04	0.05	0.036
7	Shaily India	0.17	0.15	0.17	0.17	0.18	0.168
8	Ind motor parts	0.12	0.12	0.2	0.16	0.17	0.154
9	Uniphos Ent	0.05	0.04	0.05	0.06	0.08	0.056
10	Grandeur Prod	0.03	0.03	0.04	0.05	0.06	0.042
11	Control print	0.25	0.23	0.23	0.26	0.27	0.248
12	Apollo Tricoat	0.29	0.34	0.33	0.29	0.31	0.312
13	Sat Ind	0.13	0.13	0.15	0.1	0.16	0.134
14	Singer India	0.11	0.12	0.12	0.13	0.19	0.134
15	Urja Global	0.1	-0.03	-0.08	0.09	0.04	0.024
16	Competent Auto	0.14	0.16	0.18	0.2	0.25	0.186
17	High Ground Ent	-0.05	0.16	0.19	0.28	0.27	0.17
18	Cravatex	0.11	0.2	0.3	0.4	0.39	0.28
19	Lahoti Over	0.09	0.13	0.14	0.14	0.14	0.128
20	Tandl Global	-0.002	0.08	0.11	0.05	0.18	0.0836
21	Bombay cycle	0.11	0.13	0.17	0.19	0.17	0.154
22	Mishka Exim	0.09	0.04	0.09	0.08	0.09	0.078
23	ABans enetrpris	0.45	0.45	0.51	0.44	0.43	0.456
24	Starlite compo	0.06	0.09	0.08	0.03	0.05	0.062
25	CCL int.	0.1	0.12	0.12	0.13	0.18	0.13
26	WH brady	-0.007	0.02	-0.04	0.05	0.07	0.0186
27	Maximaa Systems	0.11	0.18	0.2	0.1	0.08	0.134
28	Mystic Electr	0.09	0.1	0.09	0.07	0.08	0.086
29	Gayatri bio	0.06	0.12	0.07	0.06	0.06	0.074
30	Empower India	0.02	0.04	0.03	0.01	0.01	0.022
	Average	0.103367	0.12	0.13	0.133667	0.146	

(SOURCE – WWW.MONEYCONTROL.COM AND EXCEL)

The researcher has examined gross profit margin of 30 Trading houses for the period of 2011-2012 to 2015-16. The summaries of gross profit margin of selected trading houses are as follows

The following table 4.34 indicates gross profit margin of sampled companies working as Trading Houses in India for the period of 2011-2012 to 2015-16.

F-Test (ANOVA) Analysis:

The researcher has applied the two-way analysis of variance (F-Test) to judge the significance variance in company - wise and year-wise gross profit margin of sampled companies working as Trading Houses in India.

Table - 4.35

Abstract of F-Test

SR.NO	SUMMARY	Count	Sum	Average	Variance
1	Adani eneterpris	5	7.44	1.488	0.17977
2	MMTC ltd	5	3.56	1.712	0.27637
3	PTC India	5	7.09	1.418	0.04102
4	Swan energy	5	6.21	1.242	0.00597
5	Andrew yule	5	7.11	1.422	0.45612
6	STC India	5	6.84	1.368	0.11372
7	Shaily India	5	5.46	1.092	0.03247
8	Ind motor parts	5	18.08	3.612	0.75937
9	Uniphos Ent	5	12.72	2.544	0.15833
10	Grandeur Prod	5	11.88	2.338	0.27523
11	Control print	5	12.03	2.406	0.25468
12	Apollo Tricoat	5	8.57	1.714	0.01638
13	Sat Ind	5	10.23	2.048	0.16523
14	Singer India	5	5.96	1.192	0.02122
15	Urja Global	5	11.43	2.288	0.22798
16	Competent Auto	5	6.02	1.204	0.25828
17	High Ground Ent	5	9.61	1.922	0.04317
18	Cravatex	5	7.59	1.518	0.03077
19	Lahoti Over	5	7.51	1.502	0.01712
20	Tandl Global	5	12.72	2.544	0.15833
21	Bombay cycle	5	11.88	2.338	0.27523
22	Mishka Exim	5	12.03	2.406	0.25468
23	ABans enetrpris	5	8.57	1.714	0.01638
24	Starlite compo	5	10.23	2.048	0.16523
25	CCL int.	5	5.96	1.192	0.02122
26	WH brady	5	11.43	2.288	0.22798
27	Maximaa Systems	5	6.02	1.204	0.25828

28	Mystic Electr	5	9.61	1.922	0.04317
29	Gayatri bio	5	11.43	2.288	0.22798
30	Empower India	5	6.02	1.204	0.25828
	Year-2011-2012	30	9.61	1.922	0.04317
	Year-2012-2013	30	7.59	1.518	0.03077
	Year-2013-2014	30	7.51	1.502	0.01712
	Year-2014-2015	30	12.72	2.544	0.15833
	Year-2015-2016	30	11.88	2.338	0.27523

(SOURCE – WWW.MONEYCONTROL.COM AND EXCEL)

Abstract of F-Test is shown in table 4.35. The summary of the results of the analysis of variance test is shown in table - 4.36.

Table - 4.36

Result of F-Test

Source of Variation	SS	DF	MSS	F-Cal. Value	5% F Limit
Companies	1.516	29	0.052	30.23	1.565322
Years	0.035	4	0.00875	5.087	2.44988
Error	0.199	116	0.00172		
Total	1.75	149			

(SOURCE – WWW.MONEYCONTROL.COM AND EXCEL)

From the Table- 4.36 it is observed that:

H_1 Calculated F-Value is statistically greater than the F-Table Value at 5% significance level. Therefore the result of the F-Test rejects the null hypothesis. So we conclude that there is significant variation among company-wise gross profit margin of sampled companies working as Trading Houses in India.

H_0 Calculated F-Value is statistically greater than the F-Table Value at 5% significance level. Therefore the result of the F-Test rejects the null hypothesis. So we conclude that there is significant Variation among year-wise gross profit margin of sampled companies working as Trading Houses in India.

❖ NET PROFIT MARGIN :

Net profit margin ratio is obtained by diving net profit by sales.

$$\text{Net profit margin ration} = \frac{\text{Net Profit}}{\text{Sales}}$$

Net profit margin ratio establishes a relationship between net profit and sales and indicates management's efficiency in manufacturing, administering and selling the products. This ratio is the overall measure of the firm's ability to turn each rupee sales into net profit. If the net margin is inadequate, the firm will fail to achieve satisfactory return on shareholder's funds. This ratio also indicates the firms capacity to withstand adverse economic conditions. A firm with a high net margin ratio would be in an advantageous position to survive in the face of falling sales prices, rising costs of production or declining demand for the product. It would really be difficult for a low net margin firm to withstand these adversities. Similarly, a firm with high net profit margin can make better use of favourable conditions, such as rising sales prices, falling costs of production or increasing demand for the product.

The researcher has examined net profit margin of 30 Trading houses for the period of 2011-2012 to 2015-16. The summaries of net profit margin of selected trading houses are as follows:

The following table 4.37 indicates net profit margin of sampled companies working as trading houses in India for the period of 2011-2012 to 2015-16.

Table - 4.37

Net Profit Margin of Sampled Trading Houses

SR.NO	Trading Houses	2011-12	2012-13	2013-14	2014-15	2015-16	Average
1	Adani Enterprise	0.005	0.01	0.02	0.02	0.02	0.015
2	MMTC ltd	0.009	0.007	0.06	0.011	0.01	0.0194
3	PTC India	0.04	0.04	0.08	0.04	0.04	0.048
4	Swan energy	0.17	0.18	0.19	0.18	0.17	0.178
5	Andrew yule	0.02	0.02	0.02	0.02	0.02	0.02
6	STC India	0.03	0.02	0.02	0.02	0.03	0.024
7	Shaily India	0.1	0.09	0.1	0.09	0.1	0.096
8	Ind motor parts	0.06	0.07	0.13	0.09	0.07	0.084
9	Uniphos Ent	0.04	0.02	0.02	0.03	0.04	0.03
10	Grandeur Prod	0.02	0.02	0.02	0.03	0.03	0.024
11	Control print	0.18	0.17	0.16	0.18	0.2	0.178
12	Apollo Tricoat	0.24	0.29	0.25	0.25	0.27	0.26
13	Sat Ind	0.08	0.07	0.08	0.07	0.11	0.082
14	Singer India	0.01	0.03	0.04	0.04	0.09	0.042
15	Urja Global	0.04	-0.09	0.03	0.04	0.04	0.012
16	Competent Auto	0.09	0.09	0.11	0.14	0.19	0.124
17	High Ground Ent	-0.07	0.08	0.12	0.13	0.13	0.078
18	Cravatex	0.03	0.11	0.16	0.23	0.23	0.152
19	Lahoti Over	0.02	0.04	0.05	0.05	0.03	0.038
20	Tandl Global	-0.03	0.03	0.05	0.02	0.06	0.026
21	Bombay cycle	0.04	0.06	0.08	0.08	0.06	0.064
22	Mishka Exim	0.07	0.02	0.06	0.04	0.05	0.048
23	ABans enetrpris	0.31	0.31	0.37	0.33	0.32	0.328
24	Starlite compo	0.01	0.04	0.05	0.002	0.01	0.0224
25	CCL int.	0.03	0.05	0.05	0.06	0.1	0.058
26	WH brady	-0.05	-0.009	-0.03	0.02	0.03	-0.0078
27	Maximaa Systems	0.02	0.07	0.1	0.03	0.02	0.048
28	Mystic Electr	0.01	0.01	0.02	0.02	0.02	0.016
29	Gayatri bio	0.26	0.07	0.03	0.03	0.02	0.082
30	Empower India	0.002	0.01	0.009	-0.001	0.002	0.0044
	Average	0.059533	0.064267	0.081633	0.0764	0.083733	

(SOURCE – WWW.MONEYCONTROL.COM AND EXCEL)

F-Test (ANOVA) Analysis:

The researcher has applied the two-way analysis of variance (F-Test) to judge the significance variance in company - wise and year-wise net profit margin of sampled companies working as Trading Houses in India. Abstract of F-Test is shown in table 4.38. The summary of the results of the analysis of variance test is shown in table - 4.39.

Table - 4.38 Abstract of F-Test

SR.NO	SUMMARY	Count	Sum	Average	Variance
1	Adani Enterprise	5	0.075	0.015	0.5405
2	MMTC ltd	5	0.097	0.0194	0.000517
3	PTC India	5	0.24	0.048	0.00032
4	Swan energy	5	0.89	0.178	0.7425
5	Andrew yule	5	0.1	0.02	0
6	STC India	5	0.12	0.024	3405
7	Shaily India	5	0.48	0.096	3405
8	Ind motor parts	5	0,42	0,084	0.00078
9	Uniphos Ent	5	0.15	0.03	0.0001
10	Grandeur Prod	5	0.12	0.024	0.3405
11	Control print	5	0.89	0.178	0.00022
12	Apollo Tricoat	5	1.3	0.26	0.0004
13	Sat Ind	5	0.41	0.082	0.00027
14	Singer India	5	0,21	0.042	0.00087
15	Urja Global	5	0.06	0.012	0.00327
16	Competent Auto	5	0.62	0.124	0.00178
17	High Ground Ent	5	0.39	0.078	0.00727
18	Cravatex	5	0,76	0.152	0.00722
19	Lahoti Over	5	0.19	0.038	0.00017
20	Tandl Global	5	0.13	0.026	0.00123
21	Bombay cycle	5	0.32	0.064	0.00028
22	Mishka Exim	5	0.24	0,048	0.00037
23	ABans enetrpris	5	1.64	0.328	0.00082
24	Starlite compo	5	0.112	0.0224	0.000449
25	CCL int.	5	0.29	0.058	0.00067
26	WH brady	5	-0.039	-0.0078	0.001119
27	Maximaa Systems	5	0.24	0.048	0.00127
28	Mystic Electr	5	0.08	0.016	0.00003
29	Gayatri bio	5	0.41	0.082	0.01027
30	Empower India	5	0.0202	0.00404	2.61405
	Year-2011-2012	30	1,786	0.059533	0.007886
	Year-2012-2013	30	1.928	0.084267	0.008728
	Year-2013-2014	30	2.449	0.081633	0.006868
	Year-2014-2015	30	2.292	0.0784	0.00678
	Year-2015-2016	30	2.5102	0.083673	0.007085

(SOURCE – WWW.MONEYCONTROL.COM AND EXCEL)

Table - 4.39 Result of F-Test

Source of Variation	SS	DF	MSS	F-Cal. Value	5% F Limit
Companies	0.874051	29	0.03014	24.07885	1.565322
Years	0.013728	4	0.003432	2.741767	2.44988
Error	0.145198	116	0.001252		
Total	1.032976	149			

(SOURCE – WWW.MONEYCONTROL.COM AND EXCEL)

From the Table- 4.39 it is observed that:

H_1 Calculated F-Value is statistically greater than the F-Table Value at 5% significance level. Therefore the result of the F-Test rejects the null hypothesis. So we conclude that there is significant variation among company-wise net profit margin of sampled companies working as Trading Houses in India.

H_0 Calculated F-Value is statistically greater than the F-Table Value at 5% significance level. Therefore the result of the F-Test rejects the null hypothesis. So we conclude that there is significant variation among year-wise net profit margin of sampled companies working as Trading Houses in India.

4.3 CONCLUSION

This chapter deals with analytical study of working capital management of sampled Trading Houses in India. Various working capital ratios are calculated and hypothesis is tested at 5% level of significance with the help of two way analysis of variance (F-test).

APPENDIX

International Peer-Reviewed Referred Journal ISSN: 2321-2160

An article on comparative study of selected trading houses in India

Nilam M. Parmar
Research scholar (PhD)
Department of commerce,
Saurashtra University, Rajkot

ABSTRACT

In this study I have describe background about trading houses and activities of trading in the domestic as well as at international level I have describe about research methodology in which I have mention universe sample and other research information. This study carries on the ratio analysis and I have selected different ratios of the selected companies in number they are 30 I have done test like ANOVA on the sampled companies.

KEY WORDS -: Trading houses, Exporter, Importer, Ratio etc

INTRODUCTION

The comparative export performance of India, on the whole, was not satisfactory. The share of
India in the total world exports fell from about 2 per cent in 1950 to 0.4 per cent in 1980. Since the mid eighties, there has, however, been some improvement. In 2012 it was 0.8 per cent and the target set by the Ministry of Commerce is one per cent by 2017. India was the 13th largest exporter in the world in 1950, but there are more than 30 countries above India now. Except for two years, in all the years Since 1951, imports were larger than exports

India has experienced balance of payments problems of varying intensity in twenty nine out of
thirty five years since the beginning of the second five year plan. The cost of India of this prolonged balance of payments problem, caused by the poor export performance has been heavy. The major drawbacks of India's export sector are lack of integrated approach; problem recognition and action lags; technological problems; high costs; poor quality image; limited R&D and marketing research; supply constraints; faceless presence of Indian products abroad; infrastructural bottlenecks; structural weakness; uncertainties, procedural complexities and institutional rigidities; and inadequacy of trade information system.

From the beginning of the second five year plan (1956-61), the foreign exchange problem began to assume serious proportions. The Government began to realize the need for vigorous export promotion. It was very clear than concentrated efforts should be made for the promotion of the export of non-traditional items like engineering goods, iron and steel, iron ore, chemical & allied products, gems and jewellery, marine products, leather & leather manufacturers etc. It was also realized that unless positive steps were taken to build up a number of merchant houses, concentrating almost exclusively on exports and capable of undertaking trade on a sustained basis, it would be impossible to complete successfully against the highly experienced and resourceful trading house of other countries. resourceful trading house of other countries.

The importance of promoting merchant houses was further underlined by the need for providing channels for the export of the products of the small scale sector.In September 1960, certain broad principles for recognition of export houses were formally adopted. The scheme of export houses has been modified a number of times thereafter.

An export house is a registered exporter holding a valid export house certificate issued by the director general of foreign trade. With a view to developing new products and new markets for exports, particularly from the small and cottage industries sector, a new scheme for the recognition of trading houses was introduced in 1981-Trading houses are special category of export houses which have demonstrated export capabilities and have facilities for testing and quality control

DEFINITIONS OF TRADING HOUSES

Trading Houses are of various types and forms. They exist in a number of countries and their activities and organization vary according to the historical background and the scenario in which they operate as well as national priorities and government policies. They are known by different names in different countries. So it is difficult to formulate a definition of Trading Houses which would be universally applicable. There are, however, resemblances in certain important aspects in the organizational structures of most of Trading Houses which make it possible for them to be analyzed as one generic entity. It is thus possible to describe activities, organization and definition of Trading Houses which would be universally applicable.

A definition that covers most cases is "Trading Houses are commercial intermediaries specialized in the long term development of trade in goods & services supplied by the other parties" they focus on exporting, importing and third country trading as their core activity and use overseas marketing organization and infrastructure as well as procurement networks to service suppliers and customers. They procure internationally and sell locally and they also procure internationally and sell internationally.They serve as commercial intermediaries between suppliers and buyers located in different countries.

Government of India has a scheme to recognize established exporters as Exports Houses, Trading House etc. Trading Houses are special category of exporters which enjoy export incentives granted by Government on exporting of goods & services.

A Trading House is defined as a registered exporter holding a valid and special category of export house certificate issued by the DGFT.

SR.NO.	TRDING HOUSES	NET WORTH	CEO /MD/FOUNDERS
1	Adani Enterpris	8.7$ billion	Gautam Adani
2	MMTC Ltd.	1.5$ billion	Ved Prakash
3	PTC Ind.	10$ million	Pawan Singh
4	Swan energy	607 cr.	Nikhil v. merchant
5	Andrew Yule	3.8$ million	Shri debases jana
6	STC India	468 cr.	Rajiv Chopra
7	Shaily	124.34 cr.	Mike Sanghvi
8	Ind motor parts	687cr.	Pawan munjal
9	Uniphos ent	1$ million	RD shroff
10	Grandeur prod	500cr.	Vijay kumar deekonda
11	Control print	320cr.	Basant kabra
12	Apollo tricoat	370 cr.	Rahul gupta
13	Sat ind	700cr.	Prashant saraogi
14	Singer india	0.5$ million	Rajeev bajaj
15	Urja global	10$ million	Honey gupta
16	Competent auto	2$ million	Raj chopra
17	High ground ent	945 cr.	Sandeep r arrora
18	Cravatex	1$ billion	Rohan batra
19	Lahoti over	12$ million	Umesh rambilas
20	Tandl global	5$ million	Vineet bagana
21	Bombay cycle	975 cr.	Chirag c.doshi
22	Mishka exim	1$ million	Rejneesh gupta
23	ABans enterpris	496cr.	Abhishek bansal
24	Starlite compo	523cr.	Arvind bharti
25	CCL int	631cr.	Akash gupta
26	WH brady	333cr.	Pavan gokulchand morarka

27	Maximaa systems	251cr.	Manoj
28	Mystic electr	436 cr	Mohit khadiria
29	Gayatri bio	368 cr.	T. Sandeepkumar reddy
30	Empower india	2.4$ million	Zulfeqar mohammad khan

RESEARCH METHODOLOGY

TITLE OF THE STUDY

To study intended to know the customer satisfaction in banking industry. Consumer perception changes according to their mood and time Scenario. So, the present study is aimed to fulfill the requirement. Why so, statement of the problem under the study that has been selected. **"AN ARTICLE ON COMPARATIVE STUDY OF SELECTED TRADING HOUSES IN INDIA"**

OBJECTIVES OF THE STUDY

To know about trading houses in India
To understand the financial ratios of selected samples
To analyzed liquidity ratio of selected samples
To analyzed working capital ratio of selected samples
To analyzed the asset ratio of selected sample during the study period

HYPOTHESES OF THE STUDY
Null hypotheses
- There is no significant difference in current ratio of the sampled companies working as trading houses in India.
- There is no significant difference in quick ratio of the sampled companies working as trading houses in India.
- There is no significant in cash ratio of the sampled companies working as trading houses in India.
- There is no significant deference in interval measure of the sampled companies working as trading houses in India.
- There is no significant difference in Networking caption ration of the sampled companies working as trading houses in India.

UNIVERSE OF THE STUDY
All the trading houses are engaged in merchant activities in India are to be a part of Universe of the study, the trading houses which engaged in trading activities which are in India are universe of the study.

SAMPLE OF THE STUDY
For this study researcher has selected 30 trading houses which are working in India for the merchandise business and involved in the trading activities in India.

SAMPLE TECHNIQUES
Researcher has selected convenient random sampling technique for the selection of the samples.

PERIOD OF THE STUDY
The present study is limited up to a period for 5 year from 2011 – 12 to 2015 – 16

SOURCES OF THE DATA

The study is based on secondary data related to the study was obtain from annual reports of a companies, magazines, journals, various bulletins and websites [moneycontrol.com, rediff.com, financialtime.com etc.]

DATA ANALYSIS
TABLE SHOWS CURRENT RATIO OF SAMPLED TRADING HOUSES

SR. NO	Trading Houses	2011–2012	2012-2013	2013-2014	2014-2015	2015-2016	Average
1	Adani Enterprise	6.03	5.68	2.72	2.91	2.98	4.06
2	MMTC ltd	1.86	1.52	1.38	1.31	1.89	1.59
3	PTC India	1.63	1.44	1.74	1.43	1.60	1.57
4	Swan energy	1.56	3.35	1.64	2.43	2.22	2.24
5	Andrew Yule	12.67	10.48	18.04	12.40	13.02	13.32
6	STC India	8.32	4.32	6.81	8.06	6.38	6.78
7	Shaily India	2.22	3.02	2.51	2.39	2.36	2.50
8	Ind motor parts	2.39	3.67	2.00	2.42	1.88	2.47
9	Uniphos Ent	10.56	9.76	6.49	6.24	6.50	7.91
10	Grandeur Prod	11.59	8.66	17.38	9.09	7.20	10.78
11	Control print	1.92	2.27	1.97	1.98	2.01	2.03
12	Apollo Tricoat	1.82	5.70	2.93	2.74	5.67	3.77
13	Sat Ind	1.77	2.85	2.59	2.77	1.81	2.36
14	Singer India	2.12	2.41	1.86	2.33	1.90	2.12
15	Urja Global	1.14	0.81	0.97	1.18	0.88	1.00
16	Competent Auto	1.09	1.03	1.30	1.42	1.12	1.19
17	High Ground Ent	1.28	0.89	1.28	1.27	0.99	1.14
18	Cravatex	0.61	0.72	0.77	0.72	0.71	0.71

		2.29	2.13	2.57	2.85	2.19	**2.41**
19	Lahoti Over						
20	Tandl Global	1.82	4.61	1.82	1.67	2.88	**2.56**
21	Bombay cycle	3.27	2.24	2.98	2.47	1.53	**2.50**
22	Mishka Exim	2.15	2.26	2.18	2.03	1.91	**2.11**
23	ABans enetrpris	2.55	8.83	2.25	3.09	2.98	**3.94**
24	Starlite compo	2.79	3.26	3.42	3.48	2.96	**3.18**
25	CCL int.	3.17	2.94	2.30	2.67	2.52	**2.72**
26	WH brady	2.75	3.45	2.39	2.28	3.14	**2.80**
27	Maximaa Systems	0.88	0.52	1.04	1.15	0.82	**0.88**
28	Mystic Electr	2.87	3.36	2.65	2.28	3.47	**2.93**
29	Gayatri bio	1.35	1.62	1.38	1.20	1.34	**1.38**
30	Empower India	1.64	0.86	1.73	1.93	1.53	**1.54**
	Average	**3.27**	**3.49**	**3.37**	**3.01**	**2.95**	

(SOURCE – WWW.MONEYCONTROL.COM AND EXCEL)

F-Test (ANOVA) Analysis:

The researcher has applied the two-way analysis of variance (F-Test) to judge the significance variance in company - wise and year-wise current ratio of sampled companies working as Trading Houses in India. Abstract of F-Test is shown in table. The summary of the results of the analysis of variance test is shown in table

SR. NO	Trading Houses	2011–2012	2012–2013	2013–2014	2014–2015	2015–2016	Average
11	Adani Enterprise	6.03	5.68	2.72	2.91	2.98	**4.06**
22	MMTC ltd	1.86	1.52	1.38	1.31	1.89	**1.59**
3	PTC India	1.63	1.44	1.74	1.43	1.60	**1.57**
4	Swan energy	1.56	3.35	1.64	2.43	2.22	**2.24**
		12.67	10.48	18.04	12.40	13.02	**13.32**

5	Andrew Yule						
6	STC India	8.32	4.32	6.81	8.06	6.38	**6.78**
7	Shaily India	2.22	3.02	2.51	2.39	2.36	**2.50**
8	Ind motor parts	2.39	3.67	2.00	2.42	1.88	**2.47**
9	Uniphos Ent	10.56	9.76	6.49	6.24	6.50	**7.91**
10	Grandeur Prod	11.59	8.66	17.38	9.09	7.20	**10.78**
11	Control print	1.92	2.27	1.97	1.98	2.01	**2.03**
12	Apollo Tricoat	1.82	5.70	2.93	2.74	5.67	**3.77**
13	Sat Ind	1.77	2.85	2.59	2.77	1.81	**2.36**
14	Singer India	2.12	2.41	1.86	2.33	1.90	**2.12**
15	Urja Global	1.14	0.81	0.97	1.18	0.88	**1.00**
16	Competent Auto	1.09	1.03	1.30	1.42	1.12	**1.19**
17	High Ground Ent	1.28	0.89	1.28	1.27	0.99	**1.14**
18	Cravatex	0.61	0.72	0.77	0.72	0.71	**0.71**
19	Lahoti Over	2.29	2.13	2.57	2.85	2.19	**2.41**
20	Tandl Global	1.82	4.61	1.82	1.67	2.88	**2.56**
21	Bombay cycle	3.27	2.24	2.98	2.47	1.53	**2.50**
22	Mishka Exim	2.15	2.26	2.18	2.03	1.91	**2.11**
23	ABans enetrpris	2.55	8.83	2.25	3.09	2.98	**3.94**
24	Starlite compo	2.79	3.26	3.42	3.48	2.96	**3.18**
25	CCL int.	3.17	2.94	2.30	2.67	2.52	**2.72**
26	WH brady	2.75	3.45	2.39	2.28	3.14	**2.80**
27	Maximaa Systems	0.88	0.52	1.04	1.15	0.82	**0.88**
28	Mystic Electr	2.87	3.36	2.65	2.28	3.47	**2.93**
29	Gayatri bio	1.35	1.62	1.38	1.20	1.34	**1.38**

30	Empower India	1.64	0.86	1.73	1.93	1.53	1.54
	Average	3.27	3.49	3.37	3.01	2.95	

(SOURCE – WWW.MONEYCONTROL.COM AND EXCEL)

Result of F-Test

Source of Variation	SS	DF	MSS	F-Cal. Value	5% F Limit
Companies	1204.739	29	41.54273	25.37215	1.565322
Years	6.56056	4	1.64014	1.001713	2.44988
Error	189.9309	116	1.637336		
Total	1401.231	149			

Calculated F-Value is statistically greater than the F-Table Value at 5% significance level. Therefore the result of the F-Test rejects the null hypothesis.

H_1 So we conclude that there is significant variation among company-wise current assets ratio of sampled companies working as Trading Houses in India.

H_0 So we conclude that there is no significant variation among year-wise current ratio of sampled companies working as Trading Houses in India.

MAJOR FINDINGS OF STUDY

F-test has carried out for data analysis and hypothesis tested at 5% significance level.

- F-Calculated value is statistically less than F-Table value at 5% significance level. Therefore the result of the F-Test accepts the null hypothesis. So we conclude that there is no significant variation among **year-wise current ratio** of sampled companies working as Trading Houses in India.
- Calculated F-Value is statistically greater than the F-Table Value at 5% significance level. Therefore the result of the F-Test rejects the null hypothesis. So we conclude that there is significant variation among **company-wise quick ratio** of sampled companies working as Trading Houses in India.
- Calculated F-Value is statistically greater than the F-Table Value at 5% significance level. Therefore the result of the F-Test rejects the null hypothesis. So we conclude that there is significant variation among **year-wise cash ratio** of sampled companies working as Trading Houses in India.
- Calculated F-Value is statistically less than the F-Table Value at 5% significance level. Therefore the result of the F-Test accepts the null hypothesis. So we conclude that there is no significant variation among **year-wise interval measure** of sampled companies working as Trading Houses in India.
- F-Calculated value is less than F-Table value. Therefore, the result of the F-Test accepts the null hypothesis. So we conclude that there is no significant variation among **year-wise net working capital ratio** of sampled companies working as Trading Houses in India.

Reference

1. Chakraborthy, S. K., *Cash Working Capital Vs. Balance Sheet Working Capital in Chakravarthy & others (Eds.)*, Topics in Accounting and Finance, Calcutta: Oxford University Press, 1976.
2. Chalapathi Rao G. V., *Finance Function in relation to Materials Management, Lok Udyog*, Vol. 9, No. 9, December 1975, and Vol. 9, No. 10, January 1976.
3. Chatterjee, Bibhas, *West Bengal: How to Lift the State Undertakings from Morass Capital*, 14 April, 1977, pp.485486.
4. Chattopadhyay, P., *Credit Management in Public Sector: Some issues*, Commerce Phamplet, 1980.
5. Chattopadhyay, P., *Why are State Undertakings in West Bengal, Languishing Capital*, 15 January, 1976, pp. 102-103 and 22nd January, 1977, pp. 129-131.
6. Cohen, J. B. and Robbins, S. M., *The finance Manager*, New York: Harper & Row Publishers, 1966.
7. Cooly, Philip, L., *Advances in Business Financial Management - A Collection of Readings*, The Dryden Press.
8. Dewing, A.S., *The Financial Policy of Corporations*, The Ronald Press Co., New York, 1953, p.686.
9. Dobler, D. W. and Lee Lemer (Jr.), *Purchasing and Materials Management*, New York: McGraw Hill, 1965.
10. Donaldson, E. R., *Corporate Finance, New York:* Ronald Press Co.,1957
11. Gerstenberg, C. W., *Financial Organisation and Management, New York*: Prentice Hall, 1959.
12. Gopalakrishnan, *Charles, Financial Organisation and Management, of business, Fourth Edition,Mumbai:* Asia Publishing House, 1960,p.295.
13. Gitman Lawerence I., *Principals of management finance, harper & row* publishers,1976.
14. Gopalkrishana,P. and Sandilya, *M. S., Inventory Management Text and Cases Delhi:* The Macmillan Company of India Pvt. Ltd. 1978.
15. Gupta, N. K., *Selectivity Approach to Inventory Control- A Case Study of Public Sector (Departmental) Enterprise, Lok Udyog*, Vol. Kill, No. 3, June 1979, pp. 27-30 and Lok Udyog, Vol. XIII, No. 4, July 1979, pp. 13-16.

Books:

I. K, M. N. (2006). *Marketing researches an applied orientation* . New delhi: Dorling Kindersley India Pvt. itd.
II. Kothari, C. (2004). *"Research Methodology Methods & Techniques".* New delhi: New Age International Publishe.
III. Pathak ,Bharti: —*Indian Financial System*, Pearson Education Pvt. Ltd – 2004
IV. Dr. N.K. Rao:- *Indian Banking System*, Advance Lerner Press -2013
V. Noltingk, B. (1965). *The Human Element in Research Management.* Amsterdam: Elsevier Publishing Company.

Websites

I. www.moneycontrol.com
II. www.indianfinance.com
III. www.nse.in
IV. www.BSE.in
V. www.survrveymonky.com

CPSIA information can be obtained
at www.ICGtesting.com
Printed in the USA
LVHW081552281022
731799LV00013B/1027

9 780340 487341